The One Thing Every Mompreneur Needs to Know

by Madeleine Davis

and

Featured Expert Contributors:

Rob Tull

Archanaa Shyam

Leah Hadley

Adrianne Larsen

Hilde S. Palladino

Pamela Pedrick

Renae Gregoire

Joanna Clark

Jamie Siv Rognstad

Lindsay Gorske

Jason Webb

Natasha Mitchell

Leona D. Mathews

Sarah Olivieri

Fay Skandsen

Jasmin Tak Shum

Susan Nelson

Ruth Stern, MA

Lisa Duerre

Lori LeCarl

Esther Shelley

Jon Cook

Julia Black

Any queries relating to this publication or author may be sent to
mdavis@bigmoneybusinessbuilder.com

ISBN 9781712399743

I'm grateful you've gotten my book!
As a thank you, I'd like to offer you an
opportunity to Pick My Brain for free!
Download your "Pick My Brain"
recorded session, chock full of business
building information and strategies:
https://bigmoneybusinessbuilder.com/yes

Table of Contents

Dedication

This book and everything else is dedicated to the 4 loves of my life: my husband, Eric, and my 3 sons, Zachary, Max, and Carson. You are my every breath. Every day is filled with awe and love for you. Thank you for making me want to do better and to be better and for being YOU. I am grateful every moment for US.

Acknowledgment and Gratitude

To my parents Leon and Marta and my siblings Anna, Lenora, and Marc: Family is everything. I'm thankful, always, for your love and support.

Thank you to my in-laws, Ira, Eleanor and Alicia. When I fell in love with Eric, you were an amazing bonus. Thank you for taking me into your beautiful family.

I'm grateful for Priscilla, Gordon, my brothers-in-law, Michael and Stephen and my nieces and nephews, Steven, Julia, Sam, Aaron, Ethan, Jesse, Dani, Marni and Jonathan.

I also want to send a huge "Thank You" to my extended family and friends. We know it takes a village to raise a child, but it also takes a village to support a mompreneur. I'm grateful for my extraordinary village.

Thank you to the head of my brand agency, Doug Crowe, who believed in my message and my mission and guaranteed my success. Your support, direction, and encouragement have been invaluable.

I believe that with the right strategies, system and support, it is possible to successfully have it all - whatever "all" is for you. Thank you for reading this book and allowing me to spread my message and my mission.

Introduction

My passion is helping mompreneurs create, grow, and develop the 6-figure business of your dreams in ways that are fast, simple, maximize your impact and make you the most money so you can stop having to go to work and start loving your work.

My mission is to show you how easy it can be to build a fun and freedom-filled financial empire from the comfort of your home!

As a Multiple #1 International Best-Selling Author, Master Life, Parenting and Business Growth Strategist, Wife and Mom to 3 children I know how hard it can be to juggle it all successfully! But I believe it doesn't have to be so hard - with the right strategies, systems and support in place - it is possible to successfully have it all!

This was my motivation to bring top experts together to share The ONE Thing Every Mompreneur Needs to Know, broken down into 5 implementable steps.

My hope is that you will get inspired, find answers, take action and see results that will help you be the best mompreneur you can be.

Want to "Pick My Brain"?
Get your 90 minute recorded session for FREE:
www.bigmoneybusinessbuilder.com/yes

Chapter 1

The Ultimate Pricing Strategy

Madeleine Davis

mdavis@BigMoneyBusinessBuilder.com

My name is Madeleine Davis. I am a multiple #1 International Best-Selling Author and a Master Business Growth Strategist. Mompreneurs, just like you, hire me to help create, grow, and develop the 6-figure business of your dreams in ways that are fast, simple, maximize your message and make you the most money so you can stop *having* to go to work and start *loving* your work. My mission is to show you how easy it can be to build a fun and freedom-filled financial empire from the comfort of your couch!

The one thing every mompreneur needs to know when she's stressed out and confused about how to price her programs or services is that understanding the essential elements of a money-making pricing strategy will dramatically increase her revenue opportunities. **Here are 5 steps to help you do that.**

STEP 1: Factor In Your Desired Outcome

So many coaches get stuck worrying that they will misprice their programs and services and either charge too much or too little. This is a valid concern, but I want you to consider that, depending on your desired outcome, the same exact program or service could be successfully priced at several different price points. What is it that you are trying to achieve? Are you wanting to attract only high-level clients to fill your VIP Level programs? If you have a suite of VIP programs that you are wanting to fill immediately, having a higher price point will automatically eliminate those that are not appropriate for that level of service. However, there are other reasons, even if you are wanting to fill your VIP suite of offers, why a lower price point may work in your favor. Are you wanting to get loads of qualified clients so that you can nurture them into a bigger offer down the road? Are you wanting a quick cash infusion (hello braces, appliances breaking down, and much-needed vacations!)? If so, you may want to charge a lower investment price so that many more people sign up. For example, let's say that you have a 4-week course that would typically be valued at $497. If your desired outcome is really to fill your $2,000 program, you may decide to offer the $497 course for only $97 in order to use it as a "feeder" for your $2,000 course. Loads of people will sign up for the 4-week course for only $97 during which time you would give them loads of value and an opportunity to see how great it is to work with you. If you are over-delivering and seeding your next program properly throughout the 4 weeks, at the end, you will be able to invite your members to join your $2,000 program and enjoy a high conversion rate. In this example, the reason you want to lower your price is to get lots of people buying because only a small portion of them will choose to buy your higher offer. That's why you need a lot of traffic.

Another reason to use a lower price point would be if your desired outcome is a quick cash infusion. It will be much easier and faster to reach your fast-money goal by closing many people at a lower price point. It stands to reason that the decision to spend $100 is made much more quickly than the decision to spend $500. However, if your desired outcome is to add an additional revenue stream and you are not using this program or service as a feeder, you can price the very same program at $497 because you don't need a large influx of people to run through the program in order to fill another program. That is, you don't need to sign up 100 clients at $100 to make $10,000 and can just sign up 20 at $500 and make the same money!

Figure out what best serves you. What is your desired outcome?

STEP 2: Factor In What Your Niche Will Pay

Your audience's interest and ability to pay are real factors in this equation. Many business coaches will tell you that if you are doing a good job selling, that your prospective clients will pull together 5 credit cards and take out a second mortgage to pay you to work with them. I completely disagree with this type of thinking and the type of coaches that are attracted to working with me would not want to bully their prospective clients or endanger their financial well-being! I prefer, instead, to have my prospective clients ask me to work with them and then enroll them into a program or service that delivers their solution and is at the right price point for them. Doesn't that sound better?

In order to be able to do this, I encourage you to be strategic and reasonable about your niche's interest and ability to pay. For example, if you are a coach with an expertise in a "soft" skill (parenting, relationships, wellness), because many people don't believe that they should be paying to learn (how to be a good parent, find a good relationship, eat well), they are not willing to invest at a higher price point. Another example might be that you are a business coach, but your niche are newbies just starting out. It's likely that a newbie just starting out will not have the money to pay you the big bucks. So, what could you do in these types of situations? When you acknowledge and factor in what your niche can and will pay, you can price your program accordingly and offer it to more people.

Be creative with your market and/or price your offer lower and work with more clients. For example, I am a high-level business coach with over 30 years of experience, and my 1:1 clients pay me north of $100k to work with them. However, I love working with coaches who have not cracked the 6-figure mark! I love being able to help them have their first 10k month. And they would love to be able to work with me and pick my brain...if only they could afford to! In this case, my niche has the interest, but not the ability to pay. If I were to spend my time making high priced offers to this niche, I would make a few sales but be unable to get traction. However, when I take this factor into consideration, I can decide to lower the investment to work with me and serve more coaches that want to grow their business. We'll cover more about that in the next step.

For now, take a moment to honestly assess this factor and answer these questions: Is your particular niche interested in your offer? What is your particular niche's ability to pay?

STEP 3: Factor In Your Deliverables
When you've figured out your desired outcome and your niche's interest and ability to pay, now is the time to consider your deliverables. Many coaches get

it wrong and start with the deliverables. However, this is a big mistake. If you start with the deliverables, you may not fulfill your desired outcome. And if your niche is not interested in what you are delivering or cannot pay, the whole point is moot! Deliverables include not just what the promise of your offer is, but what is actually included in the offer. So, the promise of your offer may be that your client will "find the love of their life within the year" or "double your sales without advertising" ...but how are you delivering that information? Here are some examples of deliverables to take into consideration:

- Will it be a digital program?
- A Livestream training?
- What is the length of time involved? (4 weeks? 3 months?)
- Is it an intensive?
- If it's an intensive, is it a LIVE or is it a virtual experience?
- Will there be a support element?
- Is it a "done for you" or "done with you" offer?
- How much individual attention will they get?
- How much access do they have to you?

In general, the more access they have to you, the closer to done for you, the more individual attention they get, the higher the price point. So, let's go back to my earlier example. I knew that my niche was interested in working with me but did not have the ability to pay the high investment rate of working with me 1:1. By changing the deliverables of access, attention, and time, I was able to create what I call a "No Brainer Offer." I launched my *Pick My Brain Year-Long Laser Coaching Program* and filled it with dozens of coaches in a matter of days. How was I able to do this? I offered coaches access to me at a price point they could easily afford. No, they don't get to work with me every day like my 1:1 clients get to do. But they do get access to me monthly for 90 minutes of high-level laser coaching for an entire year to get their business-building questions answered and they can listen in as I answer other members' questions, too! At only a few hundred dollars a month, almost everyone is a quick YES. It didn't take long for me to get to that 6 figure number because every time I had a call with someone who could NOT afford my 1:1 *Unlimited Laser Coaching Program,* I was able to easily enroll them into my *Pick My Brain Laser Group program!*

Can you see that by adjusting the deliverables, I could lower the price point while still quickly reaching my financial objective and serving my niche? Talk about an all-around win! And, of course, as more and more coaches join the program, and as the investment to join the program increases, this revenue stream will continue to increase, while the deliverable—in this case, the 90-minute laser coaching session—stays the same!

Now, as a high-level Master Business Growth Strategist that can easily price that program at thousands of dollars a month instead of hundreds, why else would it be a smart choice to choose the lower price point for my Pick My Brain Year Long Laser Program? Because it also acts as a "feeder" to my higher-level programs. Remember that we talked about desired outcomes in Step 1. Well, one of my desired outcomes is to have a steady flow of applicants for my higher-level programs. Consider that at a few hundred dollars a month, most coaches making even a few thousand a month will be able to afford to join the monthly program. Once they are enrolled in the program, they are starting to use the strategies I give them to grow their business, and they get a TASTE of what it would be like to work with me in a more intensive way.

So, my *Pick My Brain Year-Long Group* meets once a month, right? When they see how much they get out of meeting with me once a month...and they start making money...can you see how they would start thinking about wanting more access to me? Of course you can! And remember that in Step 2 we talked about interest and ability to pay, right? Now, in Step 3, it's time for me to consider what deliverables I could change to make an offer to interested coaches who COULD pay more. I decided to double the access to me by offering to meet twice a month and limiting the membership, thereby increasing individual attention. Lastly, I included a "done with you element" so that I could screen-share, revise, and edit their work in real time. Of course, I needed to increase the investment as the deliverable increased, but as my coaches were already meeting their financial goals, my *Done with You Pick My Brain Mastermind* became a No Brainer Offer. And you can see that we can take this one step further...my masterminders have more access to me and see that having my eyes directly on their business makes them even MORE money and makes them want to re-invest some of that money into working with me at an even deeper level. When they see what they can accomplish working with me twice a month in a group of 10, can you see that they will start envisioning what they can accomplish if they meet with me every day and have me completely to themselves? Guess what? We are back to my high-end offer—my *1:1 Unlimited Laser Coaching Program*. And of course, at this point, they are interested and have the ability to pay the higher investment that the increased deliverable (access to me every day) demands. Can you see how factoring in deliverables has a direct impact on your pricing strategy?

Take some time now and consider all the deliverables you do and do not want to include in your offer.

STEP 4: Factor In Your Mindset

You may not be aware of how important your mindset is, but believe me, it is either going to help you or hurt you. This is an important factor in your pricing formula, and you are going to have to get real about where you are RIGHT NOW. Why? Mindset is definitely something you can work on and you can absolutely CHANGE your mindset! I work with mompreneurs all the time on this, and it is amazing what can happen for you once you DO change your mindset. But if you are NOT there yet...if you do not have a great money mindset, just because a program or service CAN sell at a higher price point, doesn't mean that YOU will be able to sell that program or service at that higher investment price! You may have to lower the price to match what you will feel comfortable selling it at, so that you don't sabotage your sales. I, of course, would like you to reach a bit. Maybe set it just outside what you feel comfortable pricing it at. But if your comfort level is selling at $500, don't try to jump to $5,000 right away. If you don't believe that you can deliver a $5,000 program or that it isn't worth $5,000, you will not be able to get anyone else to believe that either. And you will waste a lot of time trying to talk people into something you don't believe in yourself. Do yourself a favor, and, until you get your mind right, lower the price and get more sign ups. As you increase your confidence and improve your mindset, you will be able to charge more. One of my clients was selling a program for $297 when she first started with me. While working with me, she was able to steadily increase the price of her program and only two years later she was selling the SAME program for $5,000! What did she change about her offer? Not much. I created a better bonus stack and had her add in a small support component which has her working only one more hour a week—but her income skyrocketed! What really changed was her mindset which allowed her to confidently invite others to work with her for $5,000.

Take the time now to get real about where you are today and align your pricing with your comfort level.

STEP 5: Factor In Your Messaging

How good are you at being able to clearly communicate your solution as it relates to your prospective client's challenge? How good are you at connecting the dots for them? This factor may not seem like it belongs in your pricing strategy, but if your message is not on point, you don't know how to connect the dots, or you are not good at doing this for them, you will have to charge less for what you do. It won't matter what your prospective client can pay or what the deliverables are. Why? Because your prospective clients won't see the VALUE in your offer at a higher price and likely won't take the chance at a higher price point. Many coaches don't consider this, but it's critical. It's possible that you can deliver on your promise and it's possible that your solution is worth a lot of money, but if prospective clients never sign up, they will never know. It's that simple.

Think about yourself when you go shopping. Have you ever seen a low-priced product you're unsure of but bought anyway because you said to yourself, "well, it's only (low price), I'll just take a chance that it works?" If that same product was priced higher, would you still take that chance? Probably not. Understand that, if you don't have your messaging nailed down, they won't take that chance either. They are already unsure that your solution will work because they won't know until they actually sign up, so if you can't connect with them with your messaging, if they don't believe that you "get them" and that you understand their challenges and how they're impacting them, you will have to lower that price point in order for them to take that chance and for you to make more of your sales.

Make a commitment to deeply understand the challenges your ideal prospective client faces and work towards clearly communicating your solution as it relates to those challenges.

I hope you can see that in my example, my mindset and messaging stayed consistent. By taking into account my desired outcome and my clients' interest and ability to pay, I was able to manipulate the deliverables to create 3 different revenue streams by providing opportunities for clients to work with me at different levels:

- Pick My Brain Year-Long Laser Coaching Program (90 minutes, 1 x a month—large group— lowest price)
- Pick My Brain Mastermind (90 minutes, 2 x a month plus Done with You component—small group—mid price)
- 1:1 Unlimited Laser Coaching Program (Daily access, Done with You/ Done For You— private 1:1—highest price)

And that's why my Ultimate Pricing Strategy is so effective!

Creating No Brainer Offers is just one of the many ways I help my clients succeed while on their quest to making 6 figures and beyond from the comfort of their home!

If you like the way I think and would like to "Pick My Brain" for FREE go to www.bigmoneybusinessbuilder.com/yes

Chapter 2

Live Your Passion

Rob Tull

rob@path2coaching.com

My name is Rob Tull. I am a success coach, and I help mompreneurs explore new paths to rediscover their passion and energy so they can decrease stress, increase success and fulfillment, and finally be able to enjoy a fully integrated career, family, and self. My mission is to help you unlock your passion and potential while maintaining a full and balanced life.

The one thing every mompreneur needs to know when she feels uninspired is that living with passion is your birthright and is absolutely possible for you. **Here are 5 steps to help you do that.**

STEP 1: Visualize Your Perfect Life

As a mompreneur, your life is hectic, and your energy is focused on conquering task after task and managing one project after another. You pour yourself into so much that you do—but are those the things you are passionate about? If not, you are not alone. Many mompreneurs describe an ache in their daily life, like the feeling of being lost or recognizing that something is missing or out of place. One of my clients described it this way: "I had a passion that was like a fire inside me, and now it's like life kept blowing it out, and there are just a few embers left, and I'm afraid they might go out altogether."

In order to find or rekindle your passion and make it a priority by living into it, you need to see it and feel it again, recalling that fire. Passion is most commonly extinguished by fear, whether that's fear of change or fear of failure. Therefore, you will need to remove your fears to let your passion reveal itself. Typically, I like to take my clients through a visualization exercise. For people that are detail oriented and have Type A tendencies, visualization can be difficult at times. If the following exercise feels cloudy or tangled in the details, obligations, and how your vision might impact others, that's a sign that your logic and sense of order is creeping in. Leave logic out of this. Put such considerations in a mental container and put it aside. This exercise is for you; not you as a mom or partner or daughter or sister or best friend. Just you.

Also, this vision is NOT a goal; it is a reality. It is a vision of your reality that will unfold when you rekindle your passion and live into it.

I'd like you to pause for a moment and center yourself with a quick grounding exercise, such as counting your breath, doing a body scan, or simply wiggling your toes in your shoes with your feet planted firmly on the ground. Now that you are fully present, and in this moment, ask yourself this: *If you had unlimited resources, and you were completely fearless with no risk of failure or disappointment, how would you choose to spend your time?*

See yourself in this safe and limitless space. What do you look like? What are you doing? Where are you? How do you feel? What is your expression? What qualities do you notice in yourself? Stay in that vision. Do you recognize anything? What do you feel in your spirit? What do you feel in your body?

Ask yourself: *What does this tell you about your passion?*

If the vision is too broad or overwhelming, or too far removed from where you are today, let go of any frustration or other emotions that come up, and simply reset. Check in with yourself and call to mind one of your favorite daydreams. When you have a moment to let your thoughts play, what do you daydream about doing? Consider what you see in this daydream and acknowledge how you feel as a result. The feeling of this reality may feel familiar because your passion, and the resulting reality, is within you. This visualization exercise taps into your innate creativity and reveals your intuition. Recognize the feelings that come from a life lived with passion and turn your attention to your past to notice those moments when passion was present in your life

STEP 2: Acknowledge Your Patterns

The feeling that welled up when visualizing your perfect life can be similar to when you are totally immersed and completely present in the midst of something you love, where you lose track of time and everything else fades into the background. Some people call it "dropping in," or "being in the zone," or "in a flow state," or even "awakened" or "alive." It refers to the sensation when you are completely connected and attuned to what you are doing in that very moment, and it is the hallmark of being at one with your passion. We cannot live continuously in a flow state completely focused on only one area because if we did, all other areas of our lives would suffer. But tapping into that flow state when beneficial to us is a gift and becomes more accessible to us when we are passionate about the activity at hand.

I'd like to give you an activity to do that will help you tap into your flow state. However, I'd like you to be mindful and avoid 2 mistakes people often make. One is that mompreneurs can get distracted and misidentify something as a passion when it is not—by focusing on activities and interests because there is a reward, such as money or recognition. Yes, a "good" mom provides for and protects her family. However, this is not about validating your role as mom (clearly you are a good mom if you are trying to improve and grow!). This is about tracking the moments that reward you with feeling alive. Second, do not consider anyone else's judgment or opinion of the activity or event. Do not identify something you think "should" generate these sensations if they do not. This is an exercise in authenticity. Do not identify your college major or your current role as something that speaks to your passion just because you think it "should" after everything you have put into it (says the former finance major with a law degree whose passion in life is helping mompreneurs find and develop their passion and purpose in their lives).

I'll be asking you to acknowledge and track certain activities and moments so that you begin to build an awareness that will be used to reveal a pattern that will point to your passion. Look back and remember times in your life where you felt the sensation of being in the flow. By acknowledging these moments in the past, you may begin to realize that you had moments in your life that were filled with passion. Use a journal to describe these moments that occurred deep in your past, before your name was "mommy" and even further back into your childhood. Connect with those moments that really mattered to you and be sure to go beyond last week, your resumé, and your social media timeline. Once you've identified the moments where you've felt most in the flow in your past, roll it forward into the here and now. Take time each day to document any of your moments that currently generate the same sensation and add those to your journal. Soon you will realize that there are patterns in your activities and experiences that ignite your passion. Is there a theme that is woven throughout these activities, such as communication, leadership, fitness, animals, helping others, etc.? Look deeper than the obvious. Consider that it might not be the specific activity or event that generates the sensation but an aspect of it that resonates with your passion. For example: It's not selecting the décor for the room; it is the act of creating a visual piece. It's not sifting through research and articles; it is solving a puzzle. It's not the trips and travel; it's the joy of discovery.

Are you surprised by your list? How does the pattern compare to your vision in step 1? Where is it aligned?

STEP 3: Celebrate Your Preparedness

You envisioned living into your passion, and you found proof in the patterns throughout your life. Now it's time to reflect on your talents, attributes, and gifts to see how you are already prepared to live into your passion. When we believe we are destined for something, we are more willing to overcome our fears in order to move forward.

I'd like to share a popular exercise that is one of my favorites because of the afterglow. Brainstorm and compile a list of your best attributes, traits, strengths, talents, gifts, and everything that makes you uniquely you. Consider doing this privately where you can inventory and bask in your awesomeness freely. You might be tempted to create this list on paper or on your phone, but please resist that urge. The most fulfilling way is to use sticky notes, writing each attribute on a separate note and posting it on a wall or mirror in the room—you'll see why later.

This is a stream of consciousness activity where you are cataloging the traits and attributes that make you feel empowered, strong, and full of potential. These are the compliments you have gotten from parents, teachers, clients, best friends, acquaintances, strangers, and even frenemies! This is the "damn, girl, you are _____!" [fill in the blank with the humongous compliment that makes you blush, but also say "hell yeah I am!"]. This is about your personality—no body image stuff. Think about identifying those talents that don't often get to stretch in day-to-day life. Be careful, though—so many mompreneurs get into the habit of discounting their strengths or being too humble. Now is not the time for that! Be bold, be proud, and own it!

When you think you have enough sticky notes stuck on your mirror, step back and celebrate the totality of you. Looking at the sticky notes should give you the sense that it's a mosaic, where your individual traits make up this amazing image of you. This exercise is a celebration of you and an affirmation of your wonderful qualities.

What did you notice as you admitted each of your strengths and talents? How do those attributes fit with your vision? How were those traits in play in acknowledging the pattern of your passion-filled moments? What are your strengths telling you about your ability to pursue a passion? Birds were not given wings to remain in cages any more than your amazing dance moves were meant to be confined to the front seat of your car when you're stuck in traffic. By the way, this list you started is never complete. This is a great exercise to come back to often throughout your life.

Once you have acknowledged your strengths and attributes, you will see challenges as opportunities. You were made for your passion and you are fully equipped to live into it. It is within reach when you call upon your innate gifts and the values that guide you, and that's our next step.

STEP 4: Embrace Your Purpose

If your talents and traits affect patterns of actions that express your passion, then your values and beliefs influence how you use those talents and traits.

Your values are an internal navigation system that help you stay on your path and also guide you to your destination. Understanding what your values are and calibrating your life to align with those values can steer you in the direction of your passions. Values give us purpose.

I'd like to share an exercise that will help you define the values that you are most aligned with. Like the prior exercise, this will involve taking inventory, but it's not necessary to wallpaper your room with sticky notes (fun, but optional). And like celebrating your preparedness through your gifts and attributes, you will list your values as you see them and as others might identify for you. Your values are your rules for life so you can be at peace with yourself. Values might be handed down from elders or formed through life lessons and desires. You might think of them as your expectations for the world, or the "if I were in charge, everyone would [fill in the blank]" (without the Queen Bee 'tude that might come up if you entertain that thought after a much needed night cap or three). Be sure to think beyond role-endorsing values, such as my family always comes first, or my children's happiness is more important than mine. The values you need to consider are your values as a human being—they are values that are consistent—regardless of the hat you are wearing, whether that's as a mom, mompreneur, wife, sister, girlfriend, best friend, etc.

For each value, consider how you define it, how you talk it, and how you walk it.

What does each value mean to you? For example, if honesty is a value you hold dear, what exactly does honesty mean to you? How do you demonstrate it and how do you look for it (or notice its absence) in others?

How do you show each value in your words? If honesty is a value, do you find yourself being honest even when it's not in your best interest, or do you catch yourself swept up in rumors or over-embellishing your status updates? What do you tell your children about your values?

How do you demonstrate each value in your actions? Again, if honesty is a value, how do you respond when your children are dishonest? What about when they are honest, but they violate your rules?

When you consider how you define each value and live by it with your words and actions, what sensations come up when your words and actions align with a value? Congruence often creates a sense of connection and oneness. There is comfort where life fits the value and the value fits life, like a well broken-in pair of jeans or a sweater that was made for curling up on a couch. We immediately know it. What purpose do these values support? How do these values fit in your vision, in your patterns, and the attributes that prepare you for this?

When you discover that you are not behaving in a way that is in alignment with your values, that incongruity can form a knot in the pit of your stomach or fuel resistance or procrastination. This is the moment of truth...do you want to use this information to make a decision to move towards living your value... or, is it possible that the value is not truly a priority for you? For example, if "self-care" was one of your values, but you work yourself to the bone and never take time for yourself, this is a good time to decide to have your behavior line up with your stated values or to admit that, actually, self-care is NOT a core value of yours. Focus on the values where you feel like you are not living in alignment AND you also want to honor that value more. How would honoring these values differently better align with your vision?

Your values are the guiding principles for your words and actions, directing them to your life's purpose and passion. The final step is consistently bringing it all into focus.

STEP 5: Proclaim Your Passion

By now it should be evident that your passion has appeared throughout your life even if you didn't recognize it at the time. To live into your passion requires a conscious approach. However, it can be difficult to be consistently mindful of an intention, which is why some people practice a mantra as a refrain or anchor to keep their intention at the forefront of their awareness and focus.

Your words can express your passion (talk it) and your actions can demonstrate your passion (walk it), but to pursue your passion (stalk it) you need to make it a conscious focus of your daily life. In this exercise, you will put words to your passion by proclaiming it to yourself in writing.

Draft a personal mission statement that expresses how you will live into your passion. Use your phone or tablet for this because you will need to refer to it often and it will be revised over time. Think about what the exercises in the first 4 steps revealed to you about how you have lived your passion up to now, and let those observations inform your description. Don't worry about format, wordiness, or readability just yet; pour your heart out in a messy and disorganized pile of words. If you were spewing your mission statement to a friend, she might respond with "wow, that was word vomit" and that's okay. You will refine this soon.

Once you've captured your thoughts, let it rest. Over the next few weeks, at first, review this statement every day and then every few days, and consider how well these words reflect your passion and how you are living into it. What are you doing to live this proclamation? What needs to change in the description? What needs to change in how you talk it, walk it, and stalk it? The purpose of this review is to begin winnowing down the description, distilling it to the purest and simplest statement of your passion. Refine the wording and remove the excess to get to the essence, like chipping away at a block of marble to expose an exquisite sculpture that is you. As you get closer to the essence of it, it will start to feel like a mantra. Ultimately, your paragraph of several interwoven truths can be simplified to a handful of words that state your truth, your passion.

You will know when you get there because it will trigger an excitement from within, a feeling of, "that's it!" The words will be your voice to focus your mind, swell your heart, and amplify your spirit. You might even find that this statement proves that your passion and you are inextricably intertwined as one. I hope you understand that it is your birthright to live an inspired and passion-filled life. The steps above will help you get started towards fulfilling your destiny.

If you are wanting more information and some next steps on your path to your purposeful life, please visit: www.path2coaching.com/mom

Chapter 3
Restorative Mom Sleep

Archanaa Shyam
archanaa@archanaashyam.com

My name is Archanaa Shyam. I am a Master Energy Healer and I help mompreneurs enjoy deep restorative sleep so they can wake up energized and ready to face the day. The goal is to navigate the daily roller coaster with ease and finally be able to maintain a calm inner power in the midst of all the chaos and uncertainty. My mission is to help mompreneurs feel safe in their body, in their homes, and on the planet so they can confidently bring in the success they desire.

The one thing every mompreneur needs to know when she's exhausted and feels like she's dragging herself through the day, is that sleep is essential to success and is within her reach. **Here are the 5 steps to help you do that.**

STEP 1: Feeling Safe In Your Body

We all know what a difference a good night's sleep can make! Most people don't know that the feeling of safety is the most important ingredient for restorative sleep. If you're not feeling safe, for any reason, the body is just not able to relax and rest.

Some reasons for feeling unsafe may be obvious, but some are more embedded in the subconscious. Here are a few starting points to look at:
- If you've had major health challenges, the body has gone through a lot of trauma
- If you've had a difficult childhood—facing bullying or lack of connection with parents/family

- If any of your family members are facing chronic health challenges and you are in a constant panic mode as you worry about them
- If you've had to face any kind of abuse in your life that has not been completely healed and released
- If the people around you are constantly draining your energy
- If there's a lot of fear or stress in different areas of your life—there is a constant conversation happening in your mind

If you resonate with any of the above, the first thing to do is to just acknowledge these thoughts. One of my favorite quotes is, "What we resist, persists!" But everything starts to change the moment we pause and acknowledge what is going on. We keep repeating patterns until we intentionally break them. The brain keeps us in the comfort of what is familiar until we train it otherwise!

Here are some suggestions to help you get started:
- If health is a cause for concern, pay attention to your body and help it heal. Think of it this way, cars and homes have to be maintained so they will function better and last longer. The same goes for our body, too!
- Establish loving and firm boundaries, so you can have better relationships with the people in your life, whether they are your clients, family, or friends.
- If fear, stress, or anger are causes of concern, there are many ways to energetically manage these emotions so you can harness the power in them. Suppressing them won't make them go away! (We'll talk more about this later.)

Look at different areas of your life that need support. Journal about them for deeper insights on what you can do to bring in positive changes. Consider creating a Vision Board to help clarify what you really want in different areas of your life. Given all the time constraints in your busy mompreneur life, I recommend getting support for faster results. You are definitely worth it.

STEP 2: You Matter! Time for Radical Self-Love

Make yourself a priority, because when you do, you'll see that sleep comes more easily to you. When you fill your own cup, you will feel calm and centered. There is a direct correlation between self-love and restful sleep. There are only two reasons why you may not be prioritizing yourself:

- You don't believe you're worth it (prior experiences reinforced over and over).
- You don't believe you can afford to do so (so many conflicting priorities).

It's time to make yourself matter. You may ask, "Why Now?" Here's my take:
- If you don't put yourself first, no one else is going to put you first.
- If you don't think you deserve the best, no one else is going to give it to you.
- If you don't work on your dream, no one else is going to make it come true for you.
- It is time to get clear on what you really, really want.
- Keep in mind, you deserve the best.
- When you make progress, you can positively impact others and live the life you love!

This simply means making time for yourself—even if it is just 5 minutes a day. As long as you make time for yourself, it doesn't matter if you choose to take that time at the same time every day or different ones. The important point is that you make the time. When you do that for yourself, you are telling yourself that you are worthy. It's amazing how this one simple decision to make time for yourself will positively impact so many different areas of your life—including sleeping better.

Some things you can do to dramatically shift how you feel:
- Acknowledge and appreciate the progress you make every day—big or tiny—they all add up!
- Get clarity on your 'Big Why'—the vision or the dream that fuels everything you do.
- Take those extra 5 minutes for yourself at least once a day—read, journal, meditate, walk, dance, listen to music, visualize, or whatever lights up your spirit.
- List 5 things you're grateful for when you wake up every morning.
- Learn to manage your emotions and mind chatter as this can be a key to success in different areas of our life.

Now is the time to decide that you matter. It's okay to be selfish in a good way. Go ahead. Just do it and stick with it. The results will delight you for the rest of your life.

STEP 3: Things To Strike Off

The first two steps focus a lot on our inner stuff and now let's take a look outside to see what we can eliminate to support better sleep.

I want you to take a hard look at what is going on in your bedroom that is not supporting restorative sleep. Here are some areas to consider:

- Do you have anything under your bed? Can you either move it or store it away? Keeping things under the bed obstructs the free flow of energy necessary for good sleep.

- Is the bed, other furniture, electronics or anything else in your bedroom either not working or broken? Get them fixed or remove them from the room—it will otherwise trap unwanted energies that disrupt sleep patterns.

- Do you have a lot of red or other very bright colors in your bedroom? Whether it's furniture or bedding—these colors are very stimulating and not relaxing. So, there's no way you can sleep. Easiest fixes are with bedding and objects in the room. Switch to more relaxing blues and greens for easier sleep.

- Look at the objects and artifacts in your home and bedroom—are there any that depict violence, war, grief or other negative emotions? Get rid of them right away.

- Avoid watching TV, watching a movie, reading books or anything that triggers intense emotions such as anger, grief, anxiety, fear, excitement, etc. before going to bed. Replace these with opportunities that allow for humor, personal development, inspiration and other positive feelings.

- If you have a TV or other electronics (WiFi, printers, etc.) in your bedroom, turn them off completely so the radiation is not affecting your body while you sleep. Keep your cell phones at least 5 feet away even if in airplane mode.

- Avoid working in your bed unless there's no other choice. When your bed is seen as a workplace, your body will have difficulty easily resting there. If your bedroom is the only option for a workspace, consider assigning a corner of the room or even a dedicated chair that signals your subconscious that you are in "work mode." Your bed should not be that space for you.

- Sometimes it is not practical, but in general, late night eating is not recommended. When you eat late at night, your body must work to digest the food. This does not allow your organs the time they need to rest while we sleep.

- If you're into essential oils and candles, watch out for artificial ingredients that do more damage than help. Switch to natural and safer sources that are good for you and the planet.
- Another area to watch out for is discussing intense or potentially argumentative topics before going to bed. Most of us are tired and may not have all the logic and reasonableness working at optimal levels before sleeping. Keep hot topic discussions from starting in the evening and save those for late morning or early evening—plan it out or schedule these conversations in and you'll be much happier!

This list will get you started, whether you do them all or start with a few, they will all make a huge difference in getting you the restorative sleep you want!

STEP 4: Things To Add On

Alrighty, let's do some fun stuff now that can help with enjoying good sleep. We've already talked about some of them in the earlier steps and now we will build on them. Add some of these to your nightly routine and feel free to add your own favorites!

- Music, music, music! I can't say enough about this. It's got to be the relaxing and soothing type. Yes to meditation music of course! There's a lot of variety out there with apps, playlists and even YouTube. Experiment to see what works for you. Let me share a secret here—I start playing relaxing music at least an hour before going to bed and that acts as a signal to my brain telling me that my bedtime routine has begun.
- Journal, or if you're not a fan of that word, then just write stuff down. Something magical happens when you write. Reflect on the key wins or takeaways of the day, express gratitude and follow it up with a statement on how you'd like the next day to unfold. If tomorrow's to-dos keep you awake, it is a good idea to just put them on paper so you can sleep—this actually works!
- Have a soothing bath or shower (also helps with self-care). Make sure the water isn't too hot—that's not good for either the skin or the hair.
- You can light a candle, diffuse essential oils, or have fresh flowers in your bedroom—all of these will shift your energy very quickly. Remember to be safe and to blow out the candles and turn off diffusers before sleeping.

- Massage and pamper yourself with oil or cream for that extra dose of self-love. Remember that ingredients matter—the more natural, the better for your body. Whatever you put on your body will be directly absorbed through your skin, so pay attention to what you're using.
- Add some soft pillows and accessories to create a cozy environment.
- Pay attention to the materials that touch your body. For your bedding and pajamas, choose natural materials that are more comfortable and supportive. Some of the artificial materials can cause static and interfere with the quality of sleep. Reading labels will help you decide what is best for you.
- Keeping crystals in your bedroom such as tourmaline and shungite can be extremely beneficial. Avoid stimulating crystals such as Clear Quartz, as these are amplifiers.
- You can create a ritual to connect with the earth and to feel its strong support flowing into your body before going to bed. One way to do this is to sit at the edge of your bed with your feet planted firmly on the floor beneath you. Take a few healing breaths, setting your intention for a high quality, restorative night's rest. Doing this type of grounding work will help your body feel safe and will help you relax more easily.

STEP 5: Managing The Daily Emotional Triggers

It is extremely challenging to master your emotions. This is not something that you will be able to master overnight. In fact, as a mompreneur, it often feels impossible as we have to keep so many balls up in the air all the time. That's why I like to focus on managing our emotions as I believe it is impossible to master them. So, how do we even get started?

Following the 80-20 rule, let's look at the biggest emotions that get in the way with our sleep —Stress, Fear and Anger.
- Stress is a silent killer causing 60% of all illnesses. Most people are unaware of how much their stress levels are triggered by external and internal factors, which oftentimes shows up as overwhelm.
- Fear—known or unknown fears stop us from making decisions. Unmade decisions add to our stress level and fear keeps us in survival and paralysis mode.
- Anger is like fire. It can make us feel like we have no control and then leaves us with regret and guilt, frustration and irritation.

Now let's look at why it is important to reprogram this emotional circuitry:

- It affects our health and well-being at every level. Imagine the difference in the quality of your sleep if you could manage your stress, fear, and anger.
- Patterns > Emotions > Beliefs > Destiny. Whether you focus on this principle or not, you are creating your outcome. If you want better sleep, you must interrupt your current pattern.
- Emotions are the fuel to living your purpose and achieving your goals. It is time to ignite them and tap into your own potential.

Let me share one thing you can do about each of these to get you started:

- Acknowledge the fear. Understand the message/lesson. Use the fear as your guide or teacher and not as a reason to stop you. In order to go from a place of pain to power, you have to cross the bridge of fear!
- When you get angry, look at what triggers you. There is always a pattern. Look for clues as if you're watching the scene as an audience member watching a movie and not as a participant or an actor in the movie. Once you know what it is, you can decide how to react. This is a great exercise for beginning to reclaim your power.
- Unfortunately, stress is a part of life. But you can better manage your stress when you watch out for triggers. Once the trigger presents itself, use a tool such as a deep breathing exercise of inhaling for 4 counts, holding your breath for 3 counts and exhaling for 4 counts, as a way to be more present and conscious and release the stress.

We've looked at ways to feel safer in our body and to prepare ourselves for a deep and relaxed sleep that ensures regenerative healing for the entire body. Radical self-love is truly the key to rapid transformation—the moment we start improving the relationship with ourselves, it changes the external for the better. Then we looked at many things we can do both in terms of additions and deletions that will contribute to quality sleep and overall well-being in the long run. Finally, we looked at emotions—the biggest piece of the puzzle—and how to manage the 3 key ones (stress, fear, and anger) so that we don't get triggered every minute of the day. These 5 steps are great best practices that will help you begin your journey for a great night's sleep!

If you'd like to learn more about how I can help you get restorative sleep so you can stay calm while having the energy you need to navigate the mompreneur rollercoaster of our lives, schedule a complimentary strategy session with me at https://archanaashyam.com/apply

Chapter 4

Divorce-Proof Your Business

Leah Hadley, AFC, CDFA, MAFF

leah@greatlakesdfs.com

My name is Leah Hadley, AFC, CDFA, MAFF. I'm the Founder of Great Lakes Divorce Financial Solutions, LLC and Chief Mom at Moms Managing Money. I help mompreneurs safeguard their business so that they can protect their income in the face of a pending divorce. My mission is to help you plan for the best but prepare for the worst. Nobody gets married thinking their marriage will end in divorce, but I don't want you to lose all that you've worked so hard for if it's possible a divorce is in your future.

The one thing every mompreneur needs to know when she's concerned that she'll lose her business during a marital division of assets is that it is absolutely possible to protect her business and retain her ownership as long as there is careful planning. **Here are 5 steps to help you do that.**

STEP 1: Gather Information

This may seem obvious, but you need to know your business inside and out. It's easy to delegate tasks we hate doing to someone else, which can mean disengagement with the important details of your business. This can lead to you not having your finger on the pulse. Every mompreneur needs to have some basic financial education to understand what's driving her income.

You can assess your business know-how by asking yourself questions such as:
- Do you know what your biggest revenue stream is?
- Do you know what your ongoing expenses are?

- Do you know what your business is worth and how that would be calculated in the marketplace?
- Does your business have any inventory, equipment or other physical assets?
- If you sold your business today, what could you get for it?
- Where did you get the money to start your business? For example, was any pre-marital money used to buy office furniture, pay rent, or set up systems?
- Is your business considered an asset or only a source of income? (If you are a service provider and you essentially are the business, you're really just self-employed. There may not be an asset value to your business.)

If you haven't already considered these questions, now is the time to get organized. Create a binder, or if you prefer to do things online, like I do, create online records that you update quarterly with your most important business information. Maintain all licensing and permit information. Have a comprehensive list of your customers with all their contact information and sales history. Maintain original signed copies of all legally executed contracts. Remember that contracts should be maintained for a period of seven years. You can have your bookkeeper or accountant keep up with this for you but make sure to connect with them once a quarter for an update. I suggest you keep clear records of any personal capital that you invested. If any of the money that you invested in the business was earned prior to the marriage or gifted to you or inherited, make sure to document where it came from. This can all be used to show that at least a portion of your business is not part of the marital estate.

STEP 2: Think Strategically

Whether you're getting divorced or not, it's important to think strategically about your business. While the best time to divorce-proof your business is before you're actually married, you really need to take these steps as soon as possible and prior to starting divorce proceedings. I know it's not the most romantic thing to think about, but it's also not romantic to work so hard to build your business and then lose half of it due to a divorce.

If you're not yet married, consider a prenuptial agreement. If your future spouse will not sign a prenup, you may need a Domestic Asset Protection Trust. Consult with an attorney to determine your best option. If you're already married, a postnuptial agreement might make sense. However, beware that postnups have not been universally upheld by the courts. Still, having the agreement in place does make your intentions for the business clear.

If having an agreement in place with your spouse isn't in the cards, consult with your business attorney regarding your operating agreement (or partnership agreement). Make sure you've included as much protective language as possible.

If there is more than one owner of your business, you will need a buy-sell agreement. A buy-sell agreement is a contract that states how an owner's share of a business may be reassigned if that owner leaves the business, passes away, or if one of the owners divorce. Some people refer to it as a buyout agreement or a business will. Regardless of what you call it, the purpose is the same. With respect to a divorce, it details what happens to a business should any owner get a divorce. The agreement can limit a spouse's ability to acquire ownership or exclude a divorcing spouse from having voting rights. It could also give you and the other partners the right to buy the interest awarded to your ex at a predetermined price.

Regardless of whether a divorce is in your future, keeping business and personal finances separate makes good business sense for a variety of reasons. In the case of a divorce, commingling business and personal expenses could hurt your settlement. If you're paying yourself $50,000 a year, but you run $200,000 of personal expenses through your business, then your income (and your business valuation) will likely come into question. Determining which expenses are business vs. which are personal adds a level of complexity that can negatively impact your settlement.

I suggest that you pay yourself a market salary. If you pay yourself something that's below the market rate, your spouse might make a case about how it has negatively impacted your family's cash flow. As a result, he may be entitled to a greater percentage of the business or a portion of future business profits.

I also suggest that if your spouse works at your business, that you pay him the market rate for his services as well. Otherwise, he could seek a bigger percentage of the business value due to his contribution during the divorce proceedings.

STEP 3: Business Continuity

It's common for businesses to suffer when the owner is facing a life-changing event such as a divorce. It can be difficult to manage all the day-to-day needs of your business when you're distracted by what's going on in your personal life.

That's why it's important to consider how your business will continue to stay afloat during this stressful time. To manage your energy during this difficult time, I suggest you prioritize your tasks and delegate what you can in order to keep your business going without becoming overwhelmed. One of the best ways to do this is to identify the areas in your business where you make the most income that require you to invest the least amount of time. Take the time now to create systems and processes that will help make everyday repeatable tasks easier and faster for you going forward.

Another strategy to ensure your business can continue during this stressful time is to have a solid passive income stream. Knowing that your business can still generate income without you at the helm can relieve a lot of financial stress. Even if you don't have something serious going on in your life, it's nice to know that you can take a vacation and you're still earning money.

Take some time to think about your business and what your priorities would be if you were dealing with a major change in your personal life. Doing this when you're focused and clear-headed could be the difference between having your business survive a major life change or watching it slip away when you're completely overwhelmed with other things.

Do you have appropriate systems in place to weather a storm? If not, make a list of where you see the risks in your business and come up with an action plan to address those risks. Even if you never face a divorce, chances are that at some point in your business life there will be a time you'll be glad you took this preparatory step.

STEP 4: Consider Creative Alternatives

If you are proceeding with a divorce, try to settle out of court if at all possible. Settling out of court gives you the greatest control over the outcome. When you allow your case to go to court, the judge has the final say about what happens to all assets, including your business. Did you know that you could actually be forced to sell your business? That's right. It may seem unfair, but it's a risk that you take when going to trial.

There are several approaches to settling out of court that you might consider. I'm an experienced mediator and a big proponent of mediation. It is statistically one of the most affordable options and allows you to maintain your privacy so that your competitors don't get access to your business finances. It also gives you significant control over the outcome. Collaborative divorce is also a great way to get the professional expertise you need while committing to avoiding the courts.

Regardless of the process you choose, when settling outside the courts, there are more opportunities for thinking outside the box and creatively dividing assets. A Certified Divorce Financial Analyst (CDFA) is your best ally when it comes to coming up with creative financial settlements. They receive significant training and continuing education on this very topic.

I always encourage my clients to focus on the big picture when negotiating assets. If your top priority is keeping your business intact without involvement from your spouse, consider which marital assets you would be willing to give up in exchange. I recognize that sometimes there aren't other assets to give up in exchange for retaining the business, but that still doesn't mean that all is lost.

Here are some real-life examples of creative settlements that I've worked on. In one case, the wife had an accounting business that was established and grew to its current size during the marriage. As a result, all of the business was considered marital property. For this particular couple, the business was by far the largest asset in the marital estate. The wife needed to give up half the value of the business to her soon-to-be-ex, but they didn't have enough other assets to cover the value. In this case, they were able to work out a property settlement note that allowed the wife to continue running her business as she had been and pay her ex his equity in the business over a period of six years. In another case, the husband and wife worked together in the business. It was an entertainment company where the husband handled the sales and the wife handled the operations. In that case, the couple decided to continue to co-own the business as they had children that they were hoping would eventually take over. The wife wanted to work somewhere else, though. They got along well enough to maintain the ownership, but they didn't want to work together on a daily basis. They agreed that the wife would train a replacement and still have some oversight on the operations but not be involved in the day-to-day management. They created a formal business succession plan with alternatives if the transition did not go as planned.

Creative settlements are only possible when you have a solid understanding of your whole financial picture. I'm not just talking about your business now. It's important to know where your family finances stand as well. If you are not currently involved in the family finances, make it a point to become involved. Attend all meetings with your accountant and your financial advisor. Ask questions and be informed. If you don't feel comfortable asking your accountant and/or financial advisor questions, then you need to change professionals immediately. If your spouse is unwilling to change, get your own. It's not ideal, but it is important that you feel confident that you're getting your questions answered.

STEP 5: Make Lemonade Out Of Lemons

As I said before, while I love helping my clients plan for the best, I also always want to make sure that they are prepared for the worst. However, even if you feel you are facing the worst and are forced to sell or close your business as a result of a divorce, you are still going to be okay.

Remember that it was your hard work, determination, and relationships that grew your business into the success it is today. Remember that you know how to succeed, and you will do so again. As the saying goes, "When life gives you lemons, make lemonade." I want to encourage you to use the opportunity as a fresh start. As a savvy mompreneur, you're not wet behind the ears. What would you do differently this time around? How can you leverage your years of knowledge, experience, and relationships to build an even more successful business?

Get creative. Think about how your industry is changing and how starting anew could put you at the forefront of innovation. Is there a complementary business that you could start that would leverage your existing audience? Take some time to think about where your industry is going. Five years from now, do you think your business will look the same as it does today? Are there product or service lines that you offer that will be obsolete? How would you do things differently if you were starting your business from scratch today?

This is a perfect time for you to think about how to everything-proof your business so you can be prepared to make lemonade in the future, if you need to. I want you to pretend that you have lost your business and are preparing to launch something new. What information from your existing business would be helpful to hit the ground running? Do you have that information documented in a way that's easily accessible to you? Or would you literally be starting from scratch?

Brainstorm what you would need in order to get things going. For example, maybe there's some contact information you should update in your cell phone or email contacts. There's no doubt that you already have a ton of information stored in your mind. This is the time for you to make sure you have everything documented digitally and correctly. I like to use this analogy, when you move into a new house, you get to put the right things in each drawer as you move in... and you are keenly aware of what is missing. Now, think about your business in this way. What do you need to have in each "drawer" and what is missing?

As a mompreneur with two businesses and three kids, I know firsthand how many different matters you have competing for your time and energy. It's so easy to put this sort of thing off. Unfortunately, in my work, I often see women waiting until it's too late to start divorce-proofing their business. While I wish you a long and happy marriage, I want you to be prepared if everything doesn't go according to plan. You can take control and divorce-proof your business today by incorporating these 5 steps.

If you'd like additional free financial resources, visit my online library at www.financialresourcelibrary.com

Chapter 5
Finding the Fun in Work

Adrianne Larsen

amlhealth81@gmail.com

My name is Adrianne Larsen and I'm a #1 International Best-Selling Author and a fun-loving Holistic Wellness Coach. Mompreneurs hire me to help them find ways to infuse their business and their home life with fun and joy. My mission is to help mompreneurs passionately embrace their multitude of life roles, create a successful and positive mindset, and have fun while doing it all.

The one thing every mompreneur needs to know when she's overwhelmed with mom guilt or bored and ready to throw in the towel and run for the hills is that she needs to add more fun to her life. **Here are the 5 steps to help you do that.**

STEP 1: Find The Fun With Your Clients

Adding more fun into your life when working with clients will benefit both you and your clients. You're working and you are fulfilling your mission. If you're going to work anyway, why not have fun? You deserve it! Go one step further, why not create that same fun-filled experience for your clients? They also deserve it! So many mompreneurs fall into the trap of the everyday grind and monotonous routine.

What if you could have fun while working with your clients? The answer is, why wouldn't you want to have fun while working with your clients! There are so many different ways to do just that, no matter what your work is. Outside of work, what is it that you like to do? Why not incorporate things that you enjoy doing while working with your clients? One of my clients loves to tell stories so she uses storytelling as she's coaching her clients to get them out of their head and help keep them moving towards the outcomes they desire. By doing so, she creates space to connect and opportunities to relate to her clients while building trust and deepening their relationship. How can you create more fun in the conversations and interactions you're involved in? Often, we avoid asking the hard questions, such as: What's not working? What can I do personally to improve this situation? What could I do differently to make this experience more enjoyable and memorable?

If you want to develop ways for your clients to have long-term success, create experiences that are memorable and filled with joy and excitement. This will keep your clients forever faithful and eager to buy your other programs and services and will help you stand out in your field of expertise. If you are dreading meeting with a client or attending another work meeting or function, take a moment to ask yourself why, and consider what you can change. If what you're doing currently isn't benefiting you, chances are it's not benefiting your clients. The truth is, if you're not having fun you are doing more damage than good, and you are actually hindering your own and your clients' results. The key to lasting success in your business and your clients' own success is by taking away parts of the client experience that are not fun. Take the time to do a daily check-in and check-out after each client interaction. Is there any part about working with your clients that was not so fun? Is there a part of your work with them that you don't like? Are there clients that you don't even enjoy working with? If you answered yes to any of these questions, then you also need to ask yourself the following questions. Why? Why are you feeling this way? Why are you continuing to do what you're doing? If something is not working, then try anything else. Don't be afraid to ask your clients for feedback and be willing to work together to implement changes. Your mission, should you accept it, is to find things you can do every day, week, month and year that bring pure joy into your life when working with your clients and bring that same quality of fun and joy into the lives of your clients.

STEP 2: Find The Fun Within Social Media

It's easy to just blurt out posts, copy, paste, and share whatever everybody else is sharing. BORING! How does doing that help you stand out in all your amazing uniqueness? How does sharing other people's quotes showcase your own true brilliance? How does it show that you're the expert in your industry? The fact of the matter is...it doesn't, it might get some likes and even some shares of its own but simply posting without a purpose is meaningless. The secret to having fun is creating true engagement. It's fun to show up as yourself while engaging with your prospective clients! In today's social media climate, people are so disconnected from each other. We are all so busy. We spend so many hours on the computer, juggling home and work, rushing here and there. Because we are so busy, we don't have the time to nurture our relationships the way we would if we could. Most people are wanting to feel connected and have a sense of belonging. Connection is a key emotion that ignites joy and meaning into our lives and just a few minutes of engagement on social media can spark that feeling of connection and belonging that so many crave.

You can create a space for you and your tribe to connect and feel safe to be who you are. The more fun you are, the more fun they will be! One mompreneur I work with puts thought and emotion into each and every post she shares. Each post is infused with her personality and the fun things she's thinking about. Don't get me wrong, this woman is all business! She's a powerhouse business coach but she's committed to maintaining the fun in her life as she builds her empire. Her tribe of fun-loving coaches eat up her posts and love her for her twisted sense of humor. And when they sign up to work with her, they know they can expect her to make sure it will be fun. By showing up this way in front of her tribe, my client is attracting her kind of client...someone who is also fun loving! You see? It is a beautiful cycle of fun attracting fun!

Unfortunately, as coaches, we are so excited to share our experiences and our offers that we bombard our followers with too much content and information. This leaves them feeling overwhelmed and paralyzed. Is that what you want? No!

We want our audience to have fun and feel good. A fun way to engage with people on social media is by asking interesting questions or creating your own personalized memes and emotional inspiring posts. This will increase your engagement which is the foundation to building a community. The main goal of creating fun and engaging posts should be to give enough information that an emotional response is created. You want your audience to be able to relate to an experience that you are sharing. Take the time to build a rapport with your audience. One of my clients said the most fun she has is when she can keep the conversation going in comments over a period of weeks! Can you imagine the relationship she is building with her people? It's almost like they are friends! And aren't friends fun? Now, don't get freaked out thinking this has to take a lot of time or become another task to do. It doesn't. In fact, that would sap the fun right out of it! A fun, easy, and free way to create personal posts is through a free app called Canva. You don't have to be a tech goddess to know how to use it! It's so simple and fun and will turn you into a creative genius and a social media guru in no time! When you think about posting, think about what you would respond to, what would make you laugh or smile and stay on your mind throughout your day? What posts inspire you to feel good inside or take action? This is the feel-good emotions you want to create for your tribe! Now go out, have fun, and build your social media community.

STEP 3: Find The Fun Breaks In Your Day

This step is often overlooked but is so important and easy for you to do! In fact, don't over complicate this at all; that's the exact opposite of what you want to do and defeats the whole purpose of this step. This is about finding time for small fun breaks throughout your day. For example, you can decide that 10 minutes before work, 10 minutes in the middle of your day, and 10 minutes when you wrap up your day will be your "fun break" time. What will you do during your fun break? Well, that depends...what's fun for you? Here are some ideas to get the ball rolling. Set the timer for 10 minutes and:

- Have a disco dance party in your own kitchen
- Chat with your friends on the phone
- Check your social media for updates
- Watch funny YouTube clips

There are limitless ways to fill your day with little bursts of joy and excitement. One of my clients works in 50-minute time blocks. That way, she has a "fun break" at the end of every work block! She uses fun breaks to boogie around her house, to call her friends, to message her kids, well...you get the idea. Basically, she is having fun all day! If you find it hard to set time aside for you to have fun, just start with one 10-minute fun break in the morning. Once this becomes a habit, and if you feel inspired to do more, go for it! Try to find new and fun little things that bring you joy throughout the day.

See how simple and fun that was?

STEP 4: Find the Fun At Work

This is similar to finding the fun with your clients, but it's not about your clients; it's about how you work with your clients. Ask yourself what you like to do outside of work. For example, if you love to travel, would you like to include a travel component when you work with your clients? Then, maybe you would like to add a retreat offer to your business! Do you like to socialize? Maybe you would like to add a wine and cheese night to your live intensives or "coffee chats" to your online group meetings. Can you see that there are so many ways that you can add fun into your work experience?

Another way to have fun is to stop doing boring stuff! Some of your boring tasks need to go away, pronto! I know, I know. It all needs to get done. I get it! But it all doesn't need to get done by you! So, I want you to make a list of all of this boring stuff that needs to get done. And I want you to really consider how much of it actually does need to get done. I bet you can cross some of the boring things off of your list. Whatever is left on your list of boring stuff, well, we need to figure out what we are going to do with that. I bet you can find somebody that you can delegate that to. It may mean that you need to pay someone to do the stuff you don't like doing. Believe me, it's worth it! You are better off signing up one new client that you will have fun with and using that money to pay someone else to do what you don't want to do! For me, I hate bookkeeping! I don't want to deal with that. I am happy to work with one more client a week and hand that money over to my bookkeeper. I love the work I do; that's fun! But I find the numbers boring. So, I crossed that off my list. What can you cross off your list either by dumping or delegating?

Hopefully, by this point, you've whittled down the boring list to just a few lonely items that are still left. Here's what I suggest you do with these. Either decide that it's ok to be bored sometimes and just do those or try to find someone to barter with. Let's say you love creating social media posts, but you find writing emails boring. I bet you can find someone that loves writing emails and hates creating social media posts! What you do should feel fun, exciting, and inspired.

STEP 5: Find The Fun All Year

This is crucial to your fun-loving success! The more you can schedule fun into your future, the better. This will keep you in a positive frame of mind, create enjoyable experiences for everyone, and give you experiences to look forward to. Creating a schedule will allow you to plan out the time you need to accomplish the tasks necessary to execute all of your fun activities. Some of your fun activities might take place 3 months from now and you may need several hours to prepare for it. If you are scheduling retreats, for example, you can't just decide one day to do it. It will require preparation and promotion. But it sure is fun planning it out and anticipating it! There are other activities that you can do without much actual preparation, but you still have to schedule them in. For example, one of my clients has a monthly "vent fest" on the last Friday of the month. On that Friday, all of her clients are invited to an online group meeting from 4-6 pm and they take turns "venting" their frustrations and commiserating with each other. It sounds like they are just complaining, but they are not! They are laughing about their trials and tribulations and it's a great way to end the month on a fun note. My client does not need to do anything to prepare for these 2 hours. She just shows up. But she does need to block out this time on her calendar, so she doesn't mistakenly schedule something else! One of the mompreneurs I work with schedules and time blocks using different colors. This is a fun way to get the creative side of her brain working. She knows that her scheduled hours for building her business are in blue, her kids' activities are in green, house-related actives are in yellow, and her favorite color purple is for her FUN. Take some time now to plan out fun things to do all year long to positively impact the way you feel on the inside, make you feel better about yourself on the outside, greatly impact the people you work with, and have a lasting effect on your long-term success in your life and your home.

Planning fun activities with your clients, in your work, in your social media, and throughout your day and blocking them into your calendar clears your mind, allows you to focus on what's important, and creates an opportunity to enhance your life and the lives of everyone you come in contact with.

Parenting can definitely have its challenging moments, running a business has its ups and downs, and it's so easy to feel torn between balancing work, family and all the elusive self-care that other mompreneurs talk about. I can help.

If you are ready to embrace your life as a rock star mompreneur, visit:
www.reallifehealthandfitness.com

Chapter 6

Money-Making Instagram Strategies

Hilde S. Palladino

Hilde@palladinomedia.no

My name is Hilde Palladino. I am an Instagram strategist and I help mompreneurs build their business via Instagram so you can stop hunting for prospects and grow your business. My mission is to help you build a highly targeted audience.

The one thing every mompreneur needs to know when she's wanting more clients is that Instagram is a goldmine when you know what to do. **Here are 5 steps to help you do that.**

STEP 1: Target Your Customer's Story

The first thing you need to understand when creating an Instagram account for your business is that the account isn't about you. It's about your target customer. It is not a place for you to showcase your products; it's a place for your target customer to find value. Understand this and you are well on your way to 'cracking the insta-code.' You will also be miles ahead of the game when you do this; most companies treat Instagram as a catalogue. They showcase their products and all their fantastic services, but nobody cares, because they're not providing any value. All they do is try to sell their stuff. What they don't realize is that none of us spend time on Social Media because we want to be sold to! The interesting point here is that we DO like to buy...it's just that we don't want to be bombarded with stuff to buy. We are on social media to find value, have a good time, unwind and relax.

So what exactly is 'value'? Generally we break it down into three categories. Value is something that inspires, teaches, or entertains us. If you can accomplish all three in one post, you have nailed it. For example, you might have an inspiring photo with a caption telling an entertaining story that teaches us something. I'm not suggesting that it is necessary to do all three in every Instagram post, but I want you to try to incorporate at least one of the three categories in every post.

In order to understand what real value is for your specific target customer, you will need to drill down to the very core of their life. You need to know them better than they know themselves. Narrow it down to one person you can talk to—the one that is most likely to love your products or services.

Here's an activity you can do to help you create an avatar of your target customer. Ask yourself questions like:

- Who is she really?
- What keeps her awake at night?
- What does she like to do on weekends?
- How does she treat herself?
- Is she happy in her own skin?
- How is her financial situation?
- What are her interests and values?

Then give her a name and a family situation so that you can understand her so well that you can provide a solution to her problems before she knows she has them.

STEP 2: Define Your Unique Story

The biggest 'secret' on Instagram, and social media in general, is that your target audience isn't interested in you. They are not interested in your products, your life, or your beautiful pictures. They are not interested in you at all. They are interested in themselves. What that means is that they don't want to see your life.

They want to see *their* life through *your eyes*.

Once you understand this very subtle but important difference, it will shape how you interact with Instagram. This is where your unique story comes in. Only you have your specific mix of skills, experiences, and life wisdom. Only you can inspire, teach, or entertain in your way. When you find the merging point of your uniqueness and your target customers' wants and needs...that's when the magic happens.

Ask yourself:
- How can I use my stories to provide value for my target audience?
- How can I make my life experiences an inspiration for her?
- How can I solve those specific problems that she's facing?

Remember that the stories we want are not the grand stories about you surviving three months on a desert island and how you learned to make nutritional juice from a sacred tree. We want the small day-to-day stories that your target customer can see herself in.

I have my client's do a simple activity to help them connect these points.
Go back to the customer avatar you created in Step One and ask yourself:
- What kind of knowledge do I have that my target customer can learn from?
- Which of her day-to-day struggles can I help her with?
- What would we talk about over coffee?
- What would we talk about over a glass of wine?
- What can I say to make her day a little bit better (business or personal)?
- How can I inspire her to take a desired action?

Create a list of possible Instagram posts around the answers to the above questions and incorporate the three value categories. Create as many posts as possible and remember to only solve or inspire one problem per post.

STEP 3: Create an Image Story

The pictures in your Instagram grid are what people use to decide if they will stop on your account or not. In fact, the 'job' of an Instagram picture is to make your target customers stop scrolling. When they do stop scrolling and go to your account, you generally have 3-5 seconds to capture their attention. If they like what they see, they might read your captions—if they also like your writing—they WILL follow you. It's as easy as that.

Your aim is to make it a 'no brainer' for people to follow you. When we land on your account, we should immediately see what your account is about and if it is of any interest to us. We should see what story you are telling. And that's why your images should tell the story you want us to see whether we look at a single image or your collection of pictures.

Are you telling the story of the mompreneur who makes the most beautiful hand-woven scarves? Or maybe the story about the mother of three that also runs an accounting business. Your pictures and captions must align with that story. Again, the most effective stories are the day-to-day snippets that we can all relate to.

Remember—people buy from people, not from companies. The aim on Instagram is to create connections and a 'know, like, and trust factor.' The easiest way for you to accomplish that is by telling personal stories in pictures and words that your target audience can relate to. Remember to include yourself in several of your Instagram pictures. That way we get to connect with YOU and not just your products. We learn who you are, why you are running your business and what's in it for us. We want real people, with real lives and authentic businesses.

Your pictures should be of high quality, but not all of them need to be professionally taken by a photographer. Smartphones have excellent cameras, and, with small tripods, you can easily take them yourself. However, don't go for the regular selfies. It's more interesting to see someone in a "moment in time." Think of what story the picture tells us. If you love getting your hands dirty while gardening, include a picture with you digging in the garden, maybe with some colorful flowers. This is much more authentic than just a picture of you smiling in front of a garden. You can then add a caption and talk about how working in the garden affects your life, your energy, your business and so on.

What can you do to bring more of your life into your business? Start brainstorming ways that can be told through pictures and jot down some day-to-day stories that your target audience can relate to.

STEP 4: Planning

Failing to plan is planning to fail. The biggest mistake I see businesses make when they start using Instagram is that they shoot the picture and write their captions as they are about to post. That will never bring you success. Instead, you should be strategic about your Instagram posts so that each one builds on the others so that you send a clear message to your target audience.

For planning I like to use the 4 Ps of Instagram:

Prepare

Unexpected and authentic stories often come from mixing your passion with what the target customer wants and needs. Brainstorm all the things your target customers would want to know when looking to buy your products. What are their objections? How can you address that ahead of time? What are the benefits of your product? Why do we need what you're offering? How can your products help? What are the stories behind your products? Why are you passionate about what you do?

Prioritize

When running a business, a lot of activities are decided ahead of time. If you know what activities, promotions, or offers you will focus on each quarter, you can create Instagram posts that build upon each other and lead to a desired outcome for that quarter. Look for those sections of the year where it's important to stand out and see what needs to be done now, and what can wait until later. If you are looking to do a lot of video, you might need to write a mini-storyboard or produce text—or you might decide to focus on photos you can easily shoot instead.

Plan

When you plan, you can save a lot of time! Sort out all your ideas and see how you can minimize your time on production. If your account is like a mini-blog, you can set aside half a day every two weeks to get as much of your writing done as possible. If you are going to a fantastic location over the weekend, you can schedule in time for a quick photo-shoot and get a month's worth of Instagram posts in a couple of hours! Be smart about your planning and look for ways to get it done fast. Do you need to set aside an hour a week to align your photo grid? Or maybe you need a weekend alone every 3 months to get your captions done. Be sure to schedule it in your calendar so that you get it done.

Produce

Always produce in bulk and stay well ahead of your posting. A quick search will produce many apps available to help you plan your grid, captions and hashtags. Decide on what part of your business and your life you think will interest your target audience the most and start brainstorming topics around this. When you create posts for at least two weeks ahead, you can limit your Instagram use to minutes a day!

STEP 5: Convert

The purpose of your Instagram profile is to connect and convert. When you build a 'know, like and trust' factor with your audience, they are much more likely to buy from you than if you just treat your Instagram account as a catalogue to browse through. As mentioned earlier—people buy from people, and we are more likely to buy from people we like and feel a connection with.

To create really good content that will actually get you customers, you need to be strategic. Decide ahead of time what you would like the account to accomplish. Then separate your posting into 4 phases and think of each sequence of 4 as a launch. A launch can be every week or twice a year. The point is to include all the 4 phases in each sequence.

The 4 Phases:

Warm-up Phase

These posts are all about showing off your lovely business. What is it about? Who are you as a person? Why should we trust you? What is unique and different about you? This phase is for creating goodwill and building a tribe of raving fans. Create tons of value for your target audience so you can establish yourself as an expert in your niche. This is something you must do all year around. Don't sell during this phase—you need to give, give, give and establish trust.

Nurture Phase

This is where you show your target customer that you care about her. You let her know that you understand her struggles and that you are familiar with the objections she might have to investing in your solution. When you have done the work creating your customer avatar and know what keeps her up at night—

this will be easy. Create posts that help her through these struggles and you will have a raving fan.

Promote Phase

The goal for this phase is to position your product as the solution to your audience's problem. Don't try to sell; just tease her with all the delicious goodness that your product can do for her. Use live videos, stories, host challenges or free workshops. This is also the phase where you use your best pictures. Remember that the most successful businesses never push the sale; instead, they create a desire to buy.

Decision-Time Phase

Having gone through the previous phases, many of your followers are now ready to buy. They know you are the expert and that you care. You have proved that you understand their problems and now they are ready to commit. This is the phase where you promote your product. Maybe you give them a really good deal, announce a deadline, or invite them to a landing page or website.

I'd like you to create a 4-phase sequence with a clear goal. Jot down a list of all the posts you need to create in order to take the customer through each of the phases. If you have ongoing promotions, divide your sequence throughout the month. Aim to provide value on most of the days. This way, you'll establish yourself as the go-to-girl, show that you solve problems, and create a desire to buy! A few posts a week showcase your products with the intention to sell.

When you know your customer avatar, create interesting posts that provide value by combining your expertise and personality, use high quality pictures that tell a story, and build your sequence of posts in the way I described, you will build a tribe of loyal followers with many who are ready to buy from you!

To learn more about how I can help you make money using Instagram, visit my website: https://palladinomedia.no/instabiz

Chapter 7

Holistic Health for Increased Energy

Pamela Pedrick RN, CHC

coachpamelapedrick@gmail.com

My name is Pamela Pedrick, and I am a Registered Nurse, Certified Health Coach and a #1 International Best-Selling Author. I help busy, stressed out mompreneurs balance their health, parenting, and business so that they can be the superstar mompreneurs that they are. My mission is to support the complicated lives of mompreneurs.

The one thing every mompreneur needs to know when she's stressed out and exhausted with no energy to accomplish all that she wants is that she needs to have strategies in place to power her through her day. **Here are 5 steps to help you do that.**

STEP 1: Get Informed

As they say, knowledge is power. First, you need to understand what is draining your energy. Though you may think it all stems from how busy life is with your kids, significant other, and all that you need to do to have a successful business, you may not realize that there are other factors impacting your energy levels. In fact, you may be unintentionally doing things that are actually draining your energy instead of giving you energy.

For example, you may be consuming too much sugar. Do you know how much sugar you are actually having? Hidden sugars are everywhere, even in foods that are marketed as healthy. Shocking, I know. Just as you need to be savvy in business, you need to be savvy when it comes to the foods you eat, especially when it comes to sugar intake. The average person consumes 95 grams of sugar a day, which equals 77 pounds of sugar a year! The American Heart Association recommends that women only consume 20 grams a day. Many are way over that. Are you one of them? You may be aware of how much sugar you put in your coffee and tea and how much sugar you personally add to your foods. But what about packaged foods? Did you know that foods that have less or no fat almost always have more sugar? They replace the fat with sugar, so it tastes better so that we continue to buy these foods. They also sneak sugar into boxed foods you buy such as crackers, bread, pasta, pasta sauce and even those "healthy cereals" many of us eat!

What about having too much caffeine? Though caffeine will give you that quick boost of energy, if you have too much caffeine, you will experience an energy crash. The more caffeine you consume throughout the day, the worse those energy crashes feel. There are foods that are not that well known for containing caffeine such as chocolate, pudding, breakfast cereals that have chocolate flavoring and even decaffeinated coffee. Believe it or not, even headache relief medications have caffeine!

What about eating breakfast? Being a mompreneur is full of busy days and weekends. You may be so pressed for time that you skip breakfast. Or maybe you skip breakfast because you are late running the kids to school or you overslept because you were up working late. Whatever the reason, if you are skipping breakfast, you are setting yourself up for an energy crisis.
Early in the morning, your body is naturally at its lowest level of energy, so it needs you to feed it to jumpstart the energy you need for your busy day.

Do you know what EMFs are? These are electric and magnetic fields that are caused by your cell phones, cell phone towers, your Wi-Fi router and microwaves that negatively affect your energy levels. If you are exposed to any of these throughout your day, they are depleting your energy. EMFs do this by causing tiredness and fatigue, as well as disturbances, such as insomnia, in your sleep. As a result, you do not get the sleep you need to support a busy schedule the next day.

Do you get enough sleep? Lack of good quality sleep causes you to wake up groggy and wanting to press that snooze button. If you toss and turn or wake up during the night for that early morning trip to the bathroom, then your sleep and energy are compromised. If you are one to press that snooze button, you are doing even more damage as it takes your brain and body four hours to rebound. Here is what happens. A sleep cycle lasts 75 to 90 minutes. When you go back to sleep after hitting snooze, your body goes back to sleep and wants to get a complete sleep cycle in. Thus, you wake up groggy, as your body is still in sleep mode, and it will be difficult to completely wake up for the next four hours.

My guidance is to think about these areas, get the information you need, and begin to eliminate or decrease the negative impact they are having on your energy.

STEP 2: Get Rid Of Energy Depleters

Now that you know what has been draining your energy, it is time to get rid of those energy depleters. Once you get rid of them or decrease them, you will see a marked difference in your energy!

Sugar:
Limit the amount of sugar you consume. Instead of reaching for those pastries, cookies, donuts, or bagels for your breakfast, eat a high protein meal instead. The typical American breakfast is full of sugar. Swap these high sugar foods for eggs, full fat Greek yogurt, or steel cut oats. Even a meal replacement shake is an easy alternative. These are just a few options for a high protein breakfast. The protein will prevent you from having that mid-morning fatigue as it revs up your metabolism.

If you tend to go for the sugary afternoon snacks, swap them for nuts and fruit. Fruits that will supply you with extra energy without the sugar crash are avocados, apples, and bananas. Brazil nuts, almonds and pistachios are great for energy. Brazil nuts are also a complete protein and are the best nut to choose. Though the fats in nuts are healthy fats, as a snack, you only want to eat about a small hand full. Just 5 to 6 nuts are enough.

Stress:
Now I know there are some stressors, like your children, that you just do not want to get rid of! However, there is a way to get rid of stress in two minutes or

less. Lowering stress is essential as it depletes your energy stores. The longer you go without addressing your stress, the more apt you are to experience severe energy issues such as adrenal fatigue. Start getting rid of stress today so you can live not only an energetic life, but a healthier one as well. The best way to do this is with diaphragmatic breathing, where you inhale all the way through your diaphragm. Many of us are shallow breathers, keeping the breath just in our chest. When you breathe all the way to your diaphragm, you are taking in more oxygen which can be used in your cells and muscles to expand your energy. A breathing technique that lowers stress and amps up your energy utilizes deep diaphragmatic breathing. The proper way to do this is to inhale slowly all the way to your diaphragm, hold it in, and then let it out slowly. Do this five times and you will notice not only a decrease in your stress, but less tension in your neck and shoulders. You can even do this when you are having some "me" time in the bathroom while your kids are knocking on the door for your attention.

Sleeplessness:

Ever have a night of tossing and turning? Do you wake up during the night and find you can't get back to sleep? Do you have trouble falling asleep? As a mompreneur, you may experience one or all of these. Yet you need to sleep so that you can parent well and run your business. Sleep is so important for our health that even the Centers for Disease Control has cautioned on the adverse effects that lack of sleep can cause. It prevents you from being focused and at the top of your game, and it also causes you to crave sugar to compensate for the lethargy you feel after a poor night's sleep. A good night's sleep is essential. In order to have this, you need to prepare your body and your brain for sleep. One way is to power down an hour before bed. This means no more working at the computer or on the cell phone and getting ready for bed. Journaling, by writing down what is on your mind, is a good way to do this as it allows your brain to empty out your stressful thoughts and emotions so you can get a better night's sleep. Settling into bed with a novel or spiritual book is also a great way to power down and prepare your tired body for sleep.

Journal your energy levels in the morning, afternoon, and evening. Take note of how you feel after you get rid of these drainers.

STEP 3: Get In Energy Amplifiers

There are a number of things that you want to add to your daily routine to amp up your energy levels. As a mompreneur, you have busy days and may be running around all day in order to accomplish your daily tasks. Do you make the time to drink enough water? Probably not. You may have heard that drinking water is important for your health. But did you know that it is also important for your energy? Water puts oxygen into your cells and muscles for an immediate boost in energy. Failure to drink enough water leads to dehydration which leads to fatigue. Even mild dehydration causes tiredness. In fact, by the time you feel like you are thirsty, you are already dehydrated! At the minimum, you should be drinking half of your body weight in ounces each day. So, if you weigh 160 pounds, you should be drinking a minimum of 80 ounces of water daily. As a mompreneur juggling as much as you do, it's possible that your activity level requires you to drink even more water in order to stay energized throughout your day.

Eating healthy, energy-empowering foods is another way to give yourself the energy you need to parent and build your prosperous business. Foods such as fresh fruits, especially avocados, blueberries, and apples are high energy foods. All of them contain fiber which slows down the release of sugar. This allows your energy levels to remain high over a longer period of time. Avocados also have healthy fat and protein which keeps your blood sugar from plummeting, resulting in less energy slumps. Quinoa is another high energy food. It has been called a superfood for its high protein, fiber, and carbohydrate content. Additionally, quinoa is high in manganese, magnesium, and folate, all of which are used in the production of energy.

Here's a quick recipe for a delicious energy smoothie that will help power you through your day:

Apple, Banana, Blueberry Energy Smoothie
- 1 apple, chopped into pieces
- 1 banana
- A handful of blueberries, frozen or fresh
- 1/2 cup of unsweetened almond milk or water
- A handful of ice

Blend all ingredients together in a blender until smooth.

Keep track of the amount of water you are drinking and increase your water intake until you are drinking at least half your body weight in ounces.

STEP 4: Get Out Of Your Head

Do you sit at a desk for the better part of the day? Do you work from home and sit on your bed or couch with your laptop out even though the workday is technically over? Do you ever feel exhausted when you put that work away for the day? This is mental exhaustion. It's not necessarily the lack of movement, it is the fact that your brain has been working, and most likely working overtime at that. This mental fatigue does make you feel physically exhausted. Add in the fact that you are most likely working longer hours if you are in the first few years of building your empire, and you are really exhausted! Furthermore, your eyes can become strained causing neck and back pain. It can even lead to headaches and migraines. Your brain and your body need a break. It is very common for mompreneurs to experience mental fatigue because you are not only running your business, you are also likely running your home. In your head you hold your schedule, your client schedule, your children's schedules, and possibly your partner's schedule. That's a tremendous amount of information. It's stressful just thinking about all of that! You need to get that information out of your head so that you can unclutter your brain and unburden yourself from all that weight.

What I suggest to my clients is that they do a brain dump of issues that are weighing them down and problems that are unresolved. Oftentimes, when these issues remain in our minds, we tend to keep them on a loop, replaying what it is we believe we need to deal with. I encourage you to write down a sentence or two which will help you stop this repetitive cycle. Once you see it on paper, you can tell yourself that you acknowledge that it's an open issue and that you will deal with it tomorrow. I also encourage my clients to review everybody's schedule at the end of each day to make sure that all activities and clients are confirmed, so that they can stop thinking about their next day. The end of your day should be a time of respite for you.

STEP 5: Get Up And Exercise

Chances are you are inside for the better part of the day. Did you know that this literally sucks your energy? Furthermore, if you are exposed to EMFs as mentioned above, you are at even more risk for feeling exhausted. Lack of sunlight, where you are not out in the sun, affects your serotonin and melatonin levels, which in turn affects how energized you are during the day.

Serotonin helps elevate your mood and your energy and it is released during daylight hours. Exposure to sunlight aids in its release in the brain. Melatonin is a hormone that helps us to fall asleep and stay asleep, thereby affecting your energy. The best way to increase the amount of these two is to be out in the sunlight without any sunscreen on. I know, you may be thinking, but what about protecting my skin from the harmful rays of the sun? Though skin cancer is indeed a concern and we should be putting on sunscreen to protect ourselves, just 5 to 10 minutes outside is all you need. Research shows that moderately elevated serotonin results in a positive mood and a calm focused mental attitude. Thus, your mood will be improved while your energy is increased. If, for some reason, you cannot actually get outside, sit by a window to reap the benefits of the sun. Serotonin also turns into melatonin. Without enough serotonin, you will lack the melatonin to help you sleep.

So, get up and move. Exercise is an important factor in increasing your energy. Optimally, you would be moving your body 30-60 minutes every day. Some of that time can be spent outdoors getting in some sunlight! If that is too much time, every little bit helps. Get up from your desk, couch, bed, or wherever you are working and make a decision to move. For example, you can decide that every hour you are sitting down, you will get up for 5 minutes and go for a short walk or do some stretching. You may not think that 5 minutes will do anything for you, but a short 5-minute break is enough to garner huge benefits, including increasing your energy! Here are some exercises you can do during that 5-minute break that will aid in loosening up those tense muscles and decrease that mental fatigue:

- Shoulder rolls: Roll your shoulders forward 10 times and then backward 10 times.

- Shoulder squeeze: Stand tall and, with your arms at your side, pinch your shoulder blades together. Hold for three to four seconds and release. Repeat 10 times.
- Forward neck stretches: Gently move your head forward with your chin toward your neck as if you were nodding. Hold this position for 10 to 15 seconds.
- Side neck stretch: Pull your head gently to the side toward one shoulder so your ear almost touches it. Hold this position for 10 to 15 seconds. Repeat this with the other side.

Pick what you will do for your movement breaks.

As a mompreneur, you have a lot of responsibility to your children and the people you are serving through your business. You must make yourself a priority. Fatigue as a result of sugar, lack of sleep and stress can affect not only your energy, but your health as well. If you're not healthy, who will raise your children, run your business and serve your clients? Just like when you fly and they instruct you to put the oxygen mask on yourself first in the event of an emergency, you must put your health first so you can be the superstar mompreneur you are destined to be. You, your family, and your business are worth it!

Download your free energy guide: http://pamelapedrick.net/energy

Chapter 8
Blog Your Brilliance

Renae Gregoire

WriterRen@gmail.com

My name is Renae Gregoire and I'm a Message Clarifier. I help mompreneurs like you learn to blog with clarity and purpose so you can share your brilliance with the world and generate leads and sales all while working from home. My mission is to help passion-fueled mompreneurs create clear business messages, stellar content, and awesome reader experiences.

The one thing every mompreneur needs to know when she's wondering how other moms manage to make money with this online business thing is how to blog with clarity and purpose. **Here are 5 steps to help you do that.**

STEP 1: Strategize

I used to hate the word "strategize." It sounded so corporate! Then, one day, one of my mentors told me that a strategy is simply a plan. I was like, "Oh. Okay!" Now I teach bloggers to "strategize" so they can throw that word out at parties. But really, the truth is that strategy, or planning, is crucial if you want your blog to actually make money so you can stay at home with your littles. (By the way, I started my freelance writing business in 2002 when my third child was born. At the time, her brothers were just 14 months old and 2.5 years old. Yes, it's possible with a lot of help from your friends!)

So, let me ask: Why do you want to blog? Is it so that the people who visit your website will find you credible? Do you want to become an influencer and sway opinions? Would you like to differentiate yourself in a crowded field, like health and wellness or spirituality? Do you plan to use your blog to grow an email list filled with raving fans? Do you want your blog to generate leads and sales? Are you blogging to improve your writing? Or, do you simply want to share your unique take on life and connect with others who live, work, and play like you do?

Nailing your "why" is an important element of your blog's strategy. After you nail it, I recommend that you "nail" it up in a place in your home where you'll see it often. One of the ways I "nail" messages important to me is to put sticky notes along the bottom edge of my monitor. Before my eyes right now I see my sticky notes that say, "What story is the reader telling herself?" and "What other people think of me is none of my business." Both of those messages help me write from an authentic place.

One of the exercises I have my clients go through is to write down their WHY, and then whittle it down to two or three sentences. If you're not sure of your reasons for blogging, journal about your uncertainty to see what arises. Keep your written WHY where you'll see it often—maybe at your desk, on your bathroom mirror, and/or on your fridge. Seeing your WHY many times each day will keep it close to your heart when you're diving deeper into planning and writing blog posts. And, if you're feeling adventurous, also capture in words what your life and business will be like when your blog succeeds. For instance, if you're blogging to become an influencer, what will your business and life be like when you reach that goal? Maybe you'll be invited to speak at local events. Perhaps you'll be invited to co-author a book or other publication. Or, maybe you'll be able to afford that part-time sitter so you can dedicate even MORE time to growing your blog and business.

STEP 2: Commit

It's one thing to decide you want to blog, and perhaps even to write a few blog posts. It's another thing altogether to commit to blogging to a particular audience at a certain frequency. Committing is like planning, but with legs that will carry you to where you plan to go.

Let's start with committing to an audience of ideal readers. Who would they be? Your ideal readers should be people you'd love to work with. They should think that what you do matters and be a pleasure to work with. If you have trouble pinpointing your ideal reader, think about the people you'd hate to work with—people who'd disrespect you or talk down to you, people who'd be slow to respond or contribute, people who'd pay only after you begged them. Looking at your readers through those dual lenses will help you sharpen your focus on the right audience.

Another part of committing is deciding how often you'll blog. How often is enough? There is no one-size-fits-all answer. I always tell my clients to blog consistently so that readers know what to expect. You can choose to blog daily, weekly, bi-weekly, or monthly. Just be honest about what you can handle. How full is your plate right now? Do you have three under three, as I had? (Those were some crazy times!) Do you work 40 hours and then come home to care for your family? You might want to aim for blogging monthly, at least to start. Another consideration: how quickly (or slowly) do you write? I'm not the fastest writer, and that can really limit me when my schedule is also filled with client work. If you can pound out a post, fast, then give the speed variable less weight. Also consider whether or not you're a perfectionist. Perfectionism can and often does affect writing speed, but it can also show itself as fear of pushing the publish button. Your post is ready to go…your finger hovers over the button…but you just can't bring yourself to press it. You'll need to get over perfectionism at some point, but if you know that's how you operate, be gentle on yourself and allow yourself extra time, especially at first.

As a former coach used to say, "S-t-r-e-t-c-h, don't splatter!" Set a goal that's just a little out of reach, but something you *could* reach if you put your mind to it. The alternative is the splatter—when you set too big of a goal and then crash when you can't complete it. The splatter is not a good look on anyone.

I suggest that you journal on the commitment questions. Who is your ideal client? How often would you have to blog to s-t-r-e-t-c-h? How would stretching in that way fit into your life? And what blog-posting frequency might make you splatter?

STEP 3: Write For Readers
To write for readers means clear, easy-to-read blog posts on topics your ideal clients want to read. But before we talk about clarity, readability, and posting topics, I want to give you a heads-up: As you're brainstorming on topics and

writing your posts, don't ever forget that *your primary goal is to serve your ideal client.* Help her. Give her useful ideas and information. Yes, you want to sell something, too, but if your entire goal is to "sell, sell, sell!" readers will know. You'll have sales breath, and readers will smell it.

With that warning out of the way, let's turn to topics, or what you'll write about on your blog. Topics can go broad and deep. For example, suppose you happen to sell a line of skincare products, and your ideal client is another mom just like you. To determine what to blog about, ask yourself: what does that mom, your ideal client, think about skincare, about the ingredients in skincare products, about other skincare companies out there? Does she need help choosing skincare products? How about applying skincare products? You can also expand to include other, related topics. Might your ideal mom also be interested in hair care? In makeup? Shoes? Handbags? You can also write about those topics, perhaps even receiving a small affiliate commission for pointing readers to products you mention. Of course, you'll need to let readers know that you'll receive a commission if they click through and purchase. Most readers won't care; if they do, they'll just search for the product on Google rather than clicking your link.

Armed with your topics, it's now time to write about them. And that's where clarity and readability come in. Both are huge topics in and of themselves; books can (and have!) been written on them. But I can tell you this: *clarity, or, rather, the lack of it, can quickly cause readers to hit the back button or close the browser tab.* The best advice I can give you on clarity is to take time to reflect. What knowledge might readers need to have before reading this blog post? What transformation do you want readers to experience after reading this blog post? What do you want readers to be able to DO after reading it? What is the one idea you want them to leave with? What is the call to action? Clear content sets readers up for success and then leads them to it.

Thanks to automated tools, readability is easier to pin down than clarity. If you use Word, then you might be familiar with its readability scores. If you don't use Word, type "readability checker" into Google and you'll find several free readability tools. Two other tests you can do yourself are to 1) scan your blog post for complex words and replace them with simpler terms, and 2) read your blog post out loud. A great example of the first test is the word "utilize." Is that word in your blog post? Yes? Are you talking about utilization rates? No? Then please, for the love of simplicity, use the word "use" instead. Reading your post out loud may be the most effective test of readability; you'll be surprised at how much your ear picks up versus your eye. Your ear is right. Trust it!

To get a better handle on readability, I suggest that you test any piece of your writing for readability—250 words will do, but 1,000 words will give you a more accurate result. Use the checker in Word or another program you use, or run it through a free, online readability checker. What does your score tell you? Would your piece be appropriate for your audience? Why or why not?

STEP 4: Be Real

The amount of content out there on any one topic is INSANE these days. Untold multitudes are blogging, and most people are saying the same things. Back to the skincare product line, imagine that 10,000 other mompreneurs sell the products online, and they're all blogging about the line. They're all posting the company's information on their blogs, talking about features and benefits, and answering common questions that prospects and clients ask. How in the world will you make YOUR blog posts stand out so that people want to buy from you, and not from the other 9,999 mompreneurs selling the same products? The answer is to be real. Be vulnerable. Infuse your personality, thoughts, feelings, experiences, and life into your posts. After all, no one else has had exactly the same life experiences as you. No one else has your exact set of interests. No one else can weave stories of your ups and downs into blog posts about skincare products.

In fact, your uniqueness is a huge differentiator whether you're selling a skincare line, legal services, or freelance writing services. Take me for example. I used to be an accountant. Then I had three little ones and couldn't take the 80-hour weeks during tax season, which led me to create my freelance writing business. Now here I am, decades later, writing this message to you. Who else can say that? No one can. In what other book could you read the very content I'm sharing right now? In no other book. This content is uniquely mine because I'm infusing it with my personality. I could be vulnerable and tell you about blog posts that bombed. I could write a piece about "brew blogging" because my husband used to brew his own beer. I could also tell you about my postcard collection, and how it gives me ideas for my blog. What other blog mentor out there could slant her posts in exactly the same way? No other blog mentor. The content is mine.

Here's a little game that will show you how fun it is to discover your unique slants. Imagine I gave you an assignment to write a blog post using inspiration from a photo on your phone and/or the word "zeal." Go ahead! Scroll through the photos on your phone to see if anything sparks an idea for a blog post. Does anything stand out? Make a mental note of it. Second, think about zeal. What does the word zeal mean to you? What are you zealous about? What are your readers zealous about? What could you write to spark the zeal vibe in your readers?

Let me share how the game plays out for me. Looking at the photos on my phone, I see several with lovely trees showing hints of fall color. I also see a photo of me and my daughter—a "me and someone-elsie," as she likes to say. She's in the back of our car, and I'm in the front passenger seat. We were driving her back to her college after fall break. Also, on my phone, I see a photo of a paper plate that used to have a piece of cake on it. All that's left now are crumbs and other cake remnants, plus a few funny stick-figure drawings my daughter and I made while letting the cake settle into our bellies. Now, how to turn zeal and/or those photos into a blog post? Well, I could write a post on how to create a sense of zeal in your blog posts. Or maybe how to use the stick figure blogging technique (there's no such technique; I just made it up!). Or how about "falling" in love with your blog? (fall … autumn…get it?) Another possibility: Want more blog shares? Serve your readers mental cake.

See how that works? You + your blog = unique, original, interesting content! Now it's your turn? What blogging ideas do the photos on your phone and the word "zeal" inspire?

STEP 5: Get Visible

Your blog post is live! Congratulations! Now it's time to get as many eyes on it as possible. One of the reasons why I love blogging is because it gives me a massive bucket of content to draw from—content I can use for my social media accounts, email newsletters, videos, and other visibility-enhancing opportunities. To show you how it might work, let's step into the shoes of a freelance photographer.

Imagine that you've just published a blog post called "5 Secrets to a Knockout Brand Photoshoot." Let the visibility activities begin! First stop, Facebook. Over five days, two weeks, or whatever time interval works for you, schedule five different Facebook posts, each one focusing on one of the five secrets, each one pointing readers to your blog post to get the other four secrets. For bonus visibility, ask your Facebook audience to share those posts. If you're into live video, hold five different Facebook Lives, each focused on one of the five secrets. Then, upload those videos to your YouTube channel. Next stop, Twitter. Schedule a 280-character blurb about each of the secrets, again pointing readers back to your blog post for the other four.

At this point, you may be thinking, "Renae, why am I pointing people back to my blog?" Well, I haven't talked about what to put in your blog posts; that's too much to cover in our limited space together. However, I can tell you that to get the most from your blog posts, you should add one or more calls-to-action in each. Depending on the topic of the blog post, you could offer a topic-related free download, free educational video series, free email course, or even a link to a topic-related paid product. The big idea is to get people to join your email list so you can nurture the ideal folks into a someday sale.

Back to that example blog post: "5 Secrets to a Knockout Brand Photoshoot." So far, you've turned that single blog post into a lot of other content for Facebook, YouTube, and Twitter. There's also Instagram and LinkedIn to consider. And any other social sites where your ideal clients hang. Then there's your email list. You can also send the blog post to your list, either a teaser summary of the post with links to <read more>, or the entire blog post, right inside the email. Finally, consider publishing your blog post on a site like, *Medium,* too. I like to say that *Medium* is where blog posts go to get discovered. Perhaps YOUR post will be discovered there as well!

How are you feeling right now? Are you inspired? Think you can handle this blogging thing? Are you at least willing to give it a try? I say go ahead! Try it! You can get started right now by writing a blog post using the techniques in this chapter and using one of the visibility methods to get eyes on it.

If you need support in creating a blog filled with unique, interesting, differentiating blog posts that readers love and share, a blog that turns prospects into real, paying clients so you can work from home, I'd love to help. Get in touch, or check out my online blogging program, Blog Your Brilliance: www.ineedcopy.com/mompreneur

Chapter 9

Get Your Kid To Sleep

Joanna Clark

contactus@blissfulbabysleepcoaching.com

My name is Joanna Clark. I am a Pediatric Sleep Expert specializing in guilt-free, gentle baby sleep coaching. I help mothers tenderly teach their children the "skills of sleep" in a loving and nurturing way so that you can get the restorative sleep you need at night to be able to show up as a powerhouse mompreneur during the day. My mission is to alleviate sleep deprivation and have mompreneurs start their day well-rested and elated after a peaceful night, knowing their child benefited from the essential sleep needed for healthy growth and development.

The one thing every mompreneur needs to know when she's overwhelmed and exhausted from lack of sleep because her child is not sleeping well, is that it is absolutely possible to solve her child's sleep struggles once and for all so that she can enjoy calm bedtimes, peaceful nights, and reliable naps. **Here are 5 steps to help you do that.**

STEP 1: Discover The Real Sleep Disruptors Hiding In Plain Sight

When we dream of being business owners and parents, nobody is naive enough to think it will be easy. Working around a baby's schedule can get unpredictable, and many parents have come to expect they will lose a good amount of sleep. A recent study conducted by Welch's revealed that moms work an average of 98 hours a week, all this time is due to juggling their professional obligations around the schedules of their children. When your child is sleeping well, you will have more free-time, focus and energy to fulfill your important business goals and dreams. However, if your sleep is disrupted by your children's sleep difficulties, imagine the toll it will take on your health and your business.

Needless to say, my dynamic, successful mompreneur clients come to me all the time and they are perplexed over their child's disruptive sleep patterns. It may look baffling on the surface, but if you just scrape a little, a medical condition or a developmental milestone may be the culprit.

A child goes through major physical and cognitive developmental milestones very rapidly. In fact, within the first 20 months of life, a child goes through ten major developmental leaps that impact the physical, mental, and emotional states of the child—often sparking crankiness, relentless crying, and clingy behavior. Every time a child has to grapple with these changes, their sleep patterns are heavily disrupted until they master the new milestones. Babies cope with the new changes in their body by waking frequently during the night, sometimes becoming wide awake in a bid to reconcile their environment with their new skills. This can cause your baby to become fussy and needy.

Another cause for disrupted sleep is underlying medical conditions. A few underlying medical conditions that commonly contribute to childrens' sleep problems are silent reflux, asthma, eczema, food or seasonal allergies, and sleep apnea.

Now that we know that milestones and medical conditions can interfere with sleep, what steps can you take? The first task is to get professional help to rule out medical conditions. Disrupted sleep will only worsen any underlying medical condition, so work with your pediatrician to manage the medical condition, and understand that it is essential for your child to sleep soundly as it is during their sleep time that healing occurs.

The second task is to track your child's development and identify when your child is in the midst of a developmental leap. Refer to books or APPS to help you keep track of their development so you know when to anticipate night and nap time struggles.

Lastly, if it is determined that there are no medical conditions or developmental leaps causing the sleep issues, then it's time to address your child's disrupted sleep patterns by leaning on pediatric sleep science and age-and-stage appropriate behavioral modification. It's important to identify the window of developmental and neurological transitions that are the optimal timeframe to reset disruptive sleep patterns and stretch sleep duration.

To help you with this, keep track of your child's developmental milestones and be prepared to offer more opportunities to practice these skills during the day.

STEP 2: Target The Perfect "Sleep Window"

For many mompreneurs, work happens in stolen moments when the child is napping or when they work a "second shift" after the child has gone to bed. Naptimes and bedtimes are crucial for the child's growth and well-being, and they are equally important for a mompreneur's sanity and professional progress. Perpetually hanging on the child's unpredictable sleep schedule can be very frustrating and time consuming.

A child's sleep requirements vary as they progress through stages of development. Children need plenty of sleep—the first nine years typically demand at least 10 to 11 hours of quality, deep, restorative night-time sleep.

Every child has a unique and optimum "sleep window," and abiding by their window is the foundation for quality sleep. Brain science says that the perfect sleep window depends on a hormone called melatonin—commonly called "the drowsy hormone." If a child falls asleep when the "sleep window" is open, i.e. when the drowsy hormone is peaking, the possibility of falling into deep, restorative sleep increases, which, in turn, reduces frequent waking.

The sleep window is directly influenced by the interval of waking time that passes between nap cycles and bedtime. If the sleep window passes without the child sleeping, the child is overtired. The overtired child is often squirmy, and unreasonably demanding. Sometimes an overtired child will act "goofy and hyper." Both are examples of typical behavior for the "wired and tired" child. Missing the sleep window is a very common cause for hyperactivity struggles during bedtime which are typically followed by frequent waking throughout the night. This is a vicious cycle because when your child is awake throughout the night, your attention is required. As a result, your bandwidth is greatly diminished and becomes irritable and desperate for your child to sleep. This frustrating cycle feeds on itself, so it is important to recognize and catch the child's sleep window accurately.

The first suggestion I have to break this cycle is to actively pursue an early bedtime. The myth that a later bedtime means a "tired" child will sleep longer and deeper is just that—a myth. The truth is the exact opposite of it—a later bedtime means missed sleep windows and an overstimulated child that resists falling asleep and has a hard time staying asleep. It also increases the possibility of your child wanting to start the day too early…like at 4:45 a.m.!

Recognizing the sleep window begins with studying your child's body cues for sleepiness. Common cues that signal the onset of the sleep window are slow movement or speech, glazed or red-rimmed eyes, blood-infused cheeks and redness above the eyebrows. On the other hand, some children are so sensitive to their sleep windows that they skip the "early sleep cues" and start to display signs when it's already too late. For example, hair twirling or ear pulling or eye rubbing and big yawns indicates a closing sleep window—not an optimal sleep window for these children. Sometimes children that are masterful at hiding their sleep cues will only show cues if they are in a dimly lit room with a full belly.

The most reliable approach to identifying your child's sleep window is to keep a sleep log for 3 to 5 days. Record the sleep cues you notice about 10-30 minutes before each nap cycle and bedtime routine and very soon you will have identified the timeframe when your child will more easily fall into a sleep cycle.

STEP 3: Your Child's Daytime Sleep Goals Might Be The "Missing Link"

Everyone agrees that sleep is fundamental to healthy cognitive and physical growth. Yet, reports say that today's children are sleeping 70 fewer minutes than children did a century ago. Do we really think children's sleep needs have gone down? No, sleep is fundamental to good health—and children need a lot of sleep. After all, infancy and childhood are periods of rapid growth and development. In fact, child sleep problems can persist into adolescence and adulthood. Studies have linked child sleep problems with learning and memory issues as well as aggressive behavior and obesity. Sometimes, problems associated with adolescence such as depression, anxiety, and drugs stem from sleep deprivation.

Simply put, children need restorative sleep for healthy cognitive and physical growth. While every age and stage has specific sleep needs, a good chunk of it happens as "daytime sleep" for newborns through age 4. To make sure children meet their quota of required sleep within a 24-hr cycle, it's important to honor daytime sleep needs just as much as the goals for nighttime sleep.

There's extensive research and documentation on age and stage-appropriate daytime sleep goals and expectations. In many cases, the daytime sleep goals are met over the course of multiple naps. For example, a baby between the ages of 6 to 9 months typically needs 3¼ to 3½ hours of daytime sleep spread between 2-3 naps. If they do not meet their daytime sleep requirements, it will be difficult to compensate for all the lost daytime sleep during their nighttime stretch which will encourage the disruptive sleep cycle all over again. Understanding your child's specific daytime and nighttime sleep goals is crucial.

The only way to meet daytime goals is by prioritizing naps. A night full of calm and restorative sleep is made possible by adequate naps through the day. To avoid skipped or inadequate naps, I recommend keeping track of all the sleeping and waking intervals of your child over a 24-hour period. Next, watch for your child's sleep window and facilitate a nap at the right time. For babies 6 months and older, it is beneficial to provide a minimum nap length of 45 minutes, which is the duration of a restorative sleep cycle. Some naps may be longer than others, but that's fine as long as you know that your child has met their age-appropriate daily "sleep goals" by the end of the day.

STEP 4: Consistency Brings Reliability And Predictability

Children thrive on patterns. They are trying to make sense of the world in every way, and they look for patterns to anticipate what comes next. Routines, which are based on patterns provide a child with a sense of security. Routines are made when we practice the same thing with consistency. The way we respond to our child's sleep patterns sets the basis for how they react and what they will come to expect the next time. Too much of a change will only lead to chaos as your child is not able to make sense of your behaviors when the pattern is disrupted. That's why it's so important to respond consistently—even in the middle of the night when you are groggy and brain-fogged. This is what is necessary to eliminate the future tears and frustration.

Many parents fall prey to inconsistency because they are exhausted, overwhelmed, desperate, confused and racked with guilt. Here are some typical examples. Sometimes mompreneurs may feed their child to sleep and then other times they try to put their child down without that feeding. The result is usually a hysterical and inconsolable baby at bedtime. Sometimes mompreneurs become so frustrated when the "sleep tactic" that used to work to get their child to go to sleep no longer works and so, out of desperation, they let their child "cry-it-out" for 15 or 30 minutes. Maybe they heard this approach might work and want to try it out but give up when their baby continues to cry and they "can't take it anymore." Consequently, they go in and pick their child up and they use a sleep prop or sleep crutch (I'll explain more in the next step) to get the child back to sleep. Can you see what it is like for your child not knowing what to expect? That's why they are crying nonstop.

Don't worry if this sounds all too familiar. It is possible to begin a practice of consistency today. Make a routine for your child during bedtime and do everything you can to follow the same pattern at the same time every night. Also, decide on a good way to respond if your child does wake up in the middle of the night. Whatever you do, keep it consistent. Remember the mantra—"consistency is key"—and bring this consistency practice and awareness to every family member who cares for the child.

STEP 5: Your Child Needs "Sleep Skills"

Parents are so utterly exhausted! Did you know that parents lose an estimated 44 days of sleep in the first year of a child's life? That is 1055 hours of lost sleep. 21% of these children will continue to suffer compromised sleep habits beyond their third birthdays. In fact, studies predict that many parents do not go back to full nights of sleep until their child is 6 years old! That's a terribly long time to be sleep-deprived! How will that affect your life and your business? How long can you continue to operate in this sleep deprived condition of brain fog and diminished energy? What do you think your productivity will be like if this continues? This is an issue that must be addressed immediately.

Children are learning new skills every day of their lives. We teach them good eating and hygiene habits and social skills—why do we assume they will learn to sleep well on their own? It's important to understand that for children 6 months to 5 years of age, sleep is a learned skill just like everything else.

And yes, just like everything else, they may form undesirable habits around sleep. It is possible for children 6 months or older to become highly dependent on negative sleep associations commonly known as "sleep crutches" or "sleep props." If a child craves or needs something in order to fall asleep or to go back to sleep—that is a sleep crutch. Sleep crutches are not necessarily bad. In fact, they work very reliably and beautifully for newborns from age 0-6 months. However, as they get older, they will need to do away with these sleep crutches in order to become independent sleepers. My guidance at this point would be to identify at what stage of readiness your child is. This will inform your ability to gently wean off of the sleep crutches so that they don't become overly dependent on you to provide soothing support at every sleep cycle.

These 5 steps can help you create a calm and consistent routine around your child's sleep so they fall asleep faster and stay asleep longer. That means that you can get the sleep you need to have the energy, focus, and productivity to support the balance of being a powerhouse mompreneur, a confident mother of an independent sleeper, and the leader of a harmonious household.

Connect with me so I can help you navigate any sleep struggles and help you teach your child the "skills of sleep" through my signature guilt-free, gentle sleep coaching process: https://www.blissfulbabysleepcoaching.com/mompreneurs

Chapter 10

Stand Out Authentically

Jamie Siv Rognstad

jamie@standoutauthentically.com

My name is Jamie Siv Rognstad and I am a Branding and Marketing Strategist. Mompreneurs hire me to identify their unique strengths so that they are no longer invisible and are able to stand out authentically in their crowded market. My mission is to show you how.

The one thing every mompreneur needs to know when they are feeling invisible to their potential clients is that there is only one you. Instead of being lost in the crowd, you can stand out easily when you are clear and committed to showing up as yourself in business. **Here are 5 steps to help you do that.**

STEP 1: Identify Your Unique Strengths

Your uniqueness is what will separate you from the crowd. When you don't know who you really are and how you want to show up, this often leads to copycat behavior. This is exactly why you risk blending into the sea of online mompreneurs. When everyone sounds the same and acts the same, why would someone choose you? Your potential clients will choose you over another, precisely because of who you are. The magic is in discovering your unique strengths and shining the spotlight on who you are and what you bring to the table. When you identify your unique strengths and are able to express them in your professional capacity, you will be well on your way to creating a brand from the inside out.

However, in the world we live in, we are accustomed to being bombarded with other people's thoughts and feelings about us. Social media and advertising messages infiltrate our every thought. Because of this, we are conditioned to live from the outside in, always using other people's experience of us as our measuring stick. This is not the best way to live and it's not a good foundation on which to build your business. It's important to be able to connect with who you are and what makes you unique. How can you differentiate yourself from others if you are trying to live up to what they think about you? Building visibility based on what other people think about you can be quite hard.

One way I guide my clients to quiet the outside noise and connect more deeply with who they are is to have them answer a series of questions to help them identify their real authentic strengths. Set some time aside to consider the following questions and use what you learn when you meet with your clients and customers. I advise you to do this without outside input because you want to really listen to your inner voice. Grab your journal and start answering these questions:

- How do you feel about change?
- Is transformation important to you?
- Are you innovative?
- Are you intuitive?
- Do you like things to be in order?
- Do you tend to challenge authority?
- How do you feel about limits and boundaries?
- Do you like to work alone, or do you like to work in a team?
- How do you feel about meeting new people and experiencing new things?
- Do you love to gather information and share it?
- Do you love to lead projects? Or would you rather lead people?
- Are you a caregiver? Do you appreciate intimate connections in your business, or is that for family and close friends?
- Were you the class clown, or were you a more serious type? What about now? Did you change?
- Are you the type of person that sees the magic in the ordinary?

STEP 2: Identify Your Authentic Excellence

At some point in your business, a coach or mentor is going to ask you the question, "What did you love to do as a kid?" This is a question that can be hard to answer, because what does playing with Legos or finger painting have to do with the business you want to build today?

But think about it this way: If you loved playing with Legos, what did you love about it? How did it make you feel? Which skills did you develop later in life because of building those houses, bridges, and imaginary worlds? Did you have an imaginary friend? How did that build your imagination and creativity? Are you an out-of-the-box thinker? Or are you more of a concrete person?

Now think about what people are always saying about you after spending time with you. It could be:

- "I always feel so good about myself when I am with you."
- "I always learn something new when I am with you."
- "I am always so happy when I am with you."

There may be no obvious reason for this at first glance, but if you think about it, there is something about you that you are actually *DOING* that is making them *FEEL* that way about you. This is your excellence.

Your excellence is yours, and only yours. It is something that is pervasive in all areas of your life. In other words, it is not business specific, but rather it is YOU specific. It is your truth. The essential point here is that it is not who you are. It's about what you do, so, we will need to identify a verb for you. As a client, one activity I would have you do is to create a sentence that would clearly communicate what it is that you do when you are operating at your best. To construct this sentence, identify a verb that expresses how you interact with your unique excellence. You can begin with words like I inspire, I ignite, I teach, I intermediate, I explore, I love. For example, I am a person who totally LOVES really deep, heart-racing transformations, and I inspire these transformations without saying or doing anything, but just by being me. So, my sentence is: I inspire transformation, authenticity, and self-confidence.

Whatever you choose, you should really feel your excellence on a deeper level, and it has to be true no matter what, where, who, and how. What is YOUR sentence? You may be a person who always ignites passion, or maybe people feel really great about themselves when they are around you. What is your specific excellence?

Stand up and declare your Unique Excellence out loud because you should feel really great when you say it. It's fine to use 1-3 words to describe your Unique Excellence. Here are some examples to get you started:

- I inspire transformation.
- I ignite passion and purpose.
- I spark romance and sensuality.

STEP 3: Identify Your Authentic Message

You have probably seen the quote, "If you stand for nothing, you'll fall for anything," and this is exactly what we want to avoid in business so that we are recognized as authentic and stand out from the crowd. Taking a stand for something is more important than you think.

You want to listen to the voice of your soul. What is the one thing that you know is true and that you would want to share with the world? If you were on a stage in front of millions of people and you could only say one sentence to impart this wisdom, what would that sentence be? This will and should be the theme of what you teach and the work that you do. This is what we focus on in this step.

Your clients pay you for a service. You may offer multiple services or many variations of your service, but what is at the root of your offerings? My authentic message is that branding comes from within. As you are reading this, can you see that my guidance always includes a component about looking inward. All of my coaching, all of my trainings, and all of my courses depend on getting clear on who you are. This is the recurring theme in my business. What is your recurring theme? Is your authentic message that business can be easier? Is this what you want your clients to understand about you and your focus? Do you find ways to make business building easier? My guidance for you is to create a sentence that clearly communicates your high-conviction idea that you are motivated to share with the world.

STEP 4: Identify Your Authentic Values

Being Authentic means, among other things, living according to your core values. These are the essence of everything you are and do in your authentic business. These are the measurement of your truth and shine in and through you.

"Nothing can dim the light that shines from within." —*Maya Angelou*

Your brand is authentic when built on the core of your soul in a way that feels true and solid to you. When everything you communicate in your business is based on those values every day, in every situation, you will stand out as authentic to everyone you speak with.

This doesn't mean you have to run around shouting out your values every day. It means that you use them as a guide for everything you do in your business— from building and communicating your brand and programs, to supporting existing clients, to interacting with potential clients. So, remember, even though compassion may be one of your personal values, it may not be the most expressed value of your business. We are, in other words, looking for your professional values, the values by which you will run your business.

Your business values are what will make your clients connect with you on a deep core level and will also make them stick to you for the long term. We all love community, the feeling of belonging, and of being part of something bigger than ourselves.

Your values are your steering wheel, your guidance, and your road map. To discover your values, think about what it is in your life that you absolutely will not compromise on. Is it your integrity, honesty, or respect for yourself and other people? Is it purity, grace, loyalty, or something else? Then think about how this applies to your business. Your ideal client must share the same core values. Here are some examples of values:

• Reliability	• Integrity	• Tradition
• Loyalty	• Optimism	• Responsibility
• Commitment	• Passion	• Love
• Honesty	• Courage	• Humility
• Compassion	• Perseverance	• Order
• Creativity	• Justice	• Humor
• Positivity	• Harmony	• Freedom
• Respect	• Balance	• Enthusiasm

Feel free to add to this list if your values aren't here.

Pick 3-5 words from the list above. Start a sentence with the words "I am" for each of your core values. Write them in big letters on a piece of paper or make a poster on canva.com. Read them out loud every single morning and make ALL of your decisions from that place.

STEP 5: Define Your Authentic Promise

What you promise your clients is important, not just to your clients, but to your brand. What you authentically promise tells your market that you are reliable and trustworthy. Your brand promise is specific and *emotional* and usually includes naming your ideal client.

Your brand guarantees an experience. Most brand promises start with, "I help." This is not really promising an experience, so I strongly suggest that you are more creative than that. First of all, most people who buy your services really don't want your "help,"—they want access to your expertise so they can help themselves. Also, helping your clients doesn't make you stand out because everybody and their mom is using that term.

Your ideal clients aren't investing in you—they are investing in themselves, through you. It's your job to make it interesting and valuable for them to do this.

Remember, your brand is an opportunity to create:

- Meaningful, thought-provoking connections with your clients.
- Focus, intention, and energy for you in building your business.

All great personal brands clearly answer these three questions:

- Who am I?
- What do I stand for?
- In what areas am I an expert or an authority?

The first thing you need to do is to think about what kind of results you bring through your coaching, programs, and services. You want to be really specific about the outcome for your client. Your brand promise is not something you ARE, it is something you DO.

When you define your brand, you realize that a brand isn't just your colors, font, website, business card, or logo—it is all of these and more. A brand is everything that relates to your business, the results you deliver, the way you communicate your business and the way you show up. Your brand is who you are and the way you identify as a business in your market; it is what people remember you as. It is your communication, the stories you tell, and the way you tie all these elements together.

Your brand develops and grows and is established in the market when you are persistently consistent. You can create a great visual brand by playing around with colors and fonts and layout. When you are your business though, you will stand out in the marketplace so much more if your brand reflects *who you are*, not only as a person, but as a professional. Branding comes from within and is built on your natural strengths, your gifts, talents, and learned skills. Standing out from the crowd requires you to dig deep, differentiate yourself from the crowd, and stand out authentically. You can do that by identifying your core strengths and talents which come naturally to you.

You can discover your Authentic Power Brand Style by taking this quiz: http://jamiesiv.com/branding

Chapter 11

Eating for Energy

Lindsay Gorske

livewellwithlindsay@gmail.com

My name is Lindsay Gorske. I'm a Wellness Coach and I help empower mompreneurs to stay healthy and live life with balance. I help overcome all-or-nothing thinking so you can stop yo-yo dieting, learn self-awareness and create the practice of being consistent so you can reach your health goals that will stick for a lifetime. My mission is to let mompreneurs know that they can have it all without sacrificing their sanity.

The one thing every mompreneur needs to know when she's feeling sluggish and dragging through her day, is that she needs to have a foundational understanding of the role food plays in being able to energize her busy life. **Here are the 5 steps to help you do that.**

STEP 1: Get Clarity

Health is often confused with weight loss. Many people mistakenly believe that a thin-looking person is in good physical condition. Nothing could be further than the truth. They may be malnourished or lacking muscle mass or exhausted or on the verge of diabetes! Health is more than just your outward appearance. A holistic approach to health applies to your mind and body. When you focus on your health, weight loss will follow, and it will be more easily sustainable. Most people get it wrong by focusing on weight loss or what they look like first and consider their health as an afterthought. When we promote a consistent set of healthy behaviors, your health becomes a lifestyle habit instead of a chore.

When people follow healthy habits for enjoyment and wellbeing rather than weight loss, they are more likely to stick to the lifestyle changes. So, what can you do today to clarify what you will change? Where is the best place to focus on first? Focus on the things that can make an impact on your end goal. The goal is to make small shifts in your day-to-day actions with small changes like eating more vegetables, reducing processed foods, drinking more water, and taking supplements.

I suggest you write down 3 things you can do this week that are small changes. For example:
- Eat veggies with lunch and dinner.
- Drink enough water (take your body weight divide it by 2 and that is how many ounces you should have every day).
- Drink a protein shake every day.

STEP 2: Optimize Eating

Stop counting calories and focus on getting healthy! That means focusing on nutrition. When you begin to understand how food impacts your body's performance, you understand why it is good for you and are able to make better choices and feel better. As mompreneurs, we need energy to handle all of the demands placed on us during the day. We have to juggle a lot. And that means that we need to be energized and focused. Poor food choices lead to sluggishness and grogginess. How can you function optimally when you are sluggish and groggy? You can't. When you feel better, you do better. So, let's focus on the quality of your food and eat until you feel full. Full does not mean stuffed! You know when you have had enough and "enough" is different for each person. So, no comparison please, you need to do you and to eat for your body. The goal is to provide your body with the nourishment it needs to allow your body to do its thing and feel great. Here are 2 things to get you started:

1. Eat a combination of fats, fiber, proteins, and greens to stay full at every meal.
2. Be aware of how you are feeling and autocorrect it.

Be kind to yourself and ditch the perfection. Practice makes confidence and it creates a new way of thinking.

STEP 3: Optimize Energy

Again, we mompreneurs have a lot to get done in our busy days and there is nothing that will derail you more than a lack of ENERGY! So many of us go right for the chips and chocolate in the middle of the day but that is the worst thing we can do when we are feeling tired! That will not boost your energy levels. We *think* that we need sugar and carbohydrates, but that's your mind playing tricks on you. What you really need to give you the "pick me up" is a combination of protein and simple carbohydrates. So, I'm not talking about pasta, bread or potatoes. I mean apple slices with peanut butter or a cheese stick and cucumber slices or almonds and turkey slices. I know how much easier it is to grab for those unhealthy options that you've become accustomed to but make the switch from chocolate and chips to these types of powerhouse snacks! When you're feeling the urge to reach for the energy depleting options, I want you to STOP and take 3 deep breaths and think about how you felt the last time you made those choices. You probably enjoyed it for the first few minutes, but quickly either beat yourself up over it or felt like you needed to take a nap. This will remind you that when you make those choices, they don't make you feel good. This will also help you to make better choices when you begin to recognize how good you feel after the better options. Lack of energy comes down to a blood sugar imbalance which is just a fancy way of saying that your body needs nutrients. When you don't give your body what it needs, it becomes difficult to control your food cravings throughout the day. You are hardwired to eat, and your hormones will seek out carbs first because they give us the quickest energy. But as you are now beginning to recognize, you will crash soon after. Balanced eating will set you free!

A great way to get started making good choices is to have healthy options readily available. Simple things like keeping hard boiled eggs and cut-up vegetables and fruits in the refrigerator are a great way to start. I always advise my clients to prepare snack packs of dried fruits and nuts to be able to quickly toss into their purse or keep at their desk. What snacks and foods can you prepare and package so that they are ready when you need them?

STEP 4: Fix Your Relationship with Food

What is the relationship you have with yourself around food? It's important to know that how you talk to yourself matters because your mind is a powerful component of personal change and personal growth. It's important that you see that you are worthy of being healthy and happy. When you beat yourself up over every food "mistake" you make, you are pushing yourself down a negative rabbit hole. You can get trapped inside your head telling yourself all kinds of stories, but I am here to tell you that you can rewrite your story and walk away from those obstacles you put in your mind. Things you might be telling yourself that are simply not true. Things like maybe you don't feel like you are a good mom or doing a good job balancing it all or maybe you don't think you should take care of yourself at all because you have so many other responsibilities. You need to BE your best in order to DO your best.

I'd like to share a strategy that can help you feel more worthy. Make a list of sentences that describe how you want to feel. Every morning, choose to read these aloud to yourself as a way of honoring your commitment to yourself. Now, it's possible that these are words that you don't necessarily feel about yourself right now. Don't worry about that. This is part of the exercise. The more you say them and commit to them, the more things will begin to change for you. Here are some examples to get you started:

- I am healthy, confident, and I feel great.
- I focus on good foods that give me energy.
- I am empowered to make changes that move me towards my goals.
- I am in control of my own actions and make smart decisions.

We all have the power to change our relationships with food. Food is often a way that we console or reward ourselves. Instead of rewarding or consoling ourselves with cupcakes, realize that when we eat real, nutritious food, we will feel better and have the energy to do what we want.

STEP 5: Stay Committed

Staying committed is easier said than done. We can go on vacation and go off the rails drinking and eating everything without thinking about the repercussions. Then it may take us a month to get back on track. Soon after, the holidays come and then there are birthdays and celebrations and it's all just a slippery slope. The thing is, eating for energy is a lifestyle commitment. It's a commitment to your life. And your life is going on all the time, whether or not you are on vacation, it's a holiday, it's your birthday or whatever you have going on. So, I'm not saying to shun your birthday cake! On the contrary, I want you to enjoy your birthday cake and, hopefully, there will be sprinkles everywhere! It's just that I want you to make a commitment to yourself to live a nutritious lifestyle with an occasional indulgence. Occasional doesn't mean every day or every week. Occasional means occasional. That means once in a while. So, if you went for the pizza this afternoon, that means that you'll make a better choice for dessert after dinner. Staying true to your commitment but flexible in your approach is really what it comes down to. Staying committed really comes down to every choice you make. But when you make an intentional choice to have, for example, a slice of cake for your birthday, or you make a choice you aren't proud of—for example, I'll have the whole cake for my birthday—your mission is to get back to better choices as quickly as possible. So that you don't continue making energy depleting choices and shift back to energy increasing choices, consider what your bigger WHY is. WHY do you want more energy? Is it to be a better mom so you can be more involved with your children? Is it so you can pay closer attention to your client conversations? Is it so you can have enough energy left over at the end of the day to indulge in one of your passions? Think about what it is you really want that energy for and remind yourself that those energy depleting foods are not going to get you what you want. One of my favorite exercises that I use with my clients is to have them identify their bigger why and then connect it to what we talked about in step 3, recognizing how our food choices make us feel. I'd like to encourage you to write a sentence that you can say to yourself when you are in this situation. For example:

Having abundant energy is important to me so that I don't snap at my children, can show up more professionally for my clients and still want to enjoy my partner's company at the end of the day, and I know that (having a box of doughnuts) isn't going to get me that so my next food choice will be a food that makes me feel great and gives me the energy to do everything I want.

What is your sentence?

Food is necessary. Your food choices greatly impact the quality of your life. You are in control of what you eat. We all need food to live, the question is, how will you choose to live? I hope that these steps have given you a foundational understanding of the role food plays in being able to balance your mompreneur's life. To learn more, visit me at:

www.BeWellandLiveWellwithLindsay.com/Ready

Chapter 12
Mastering Email Marketing

Jason Webb
jason@followupfuel.com

My name is Jason Webb. I am an internet marketer and I help mompreneurs with email marketing so they can stop struggling to increase sales and grow their businesses. My mission is to teach you how to do that through email marketing.

The one thing every mompreneur needs to know when she's confused about how to increase sales is to understand the foundations of email marketing. **Here are the 5 steps to help you do that.**

STEP 1: Give Your Visitors A Place to Land

For any online business, website visitors are an important goal just like foot traffic for a brick-and-mortar store. However, in a physical store, visitors are more likely to convert because they have taken the effort to visit the store. Online visitors are used to surfing the internet and jumping quickly from page to page. They could visit your website and bounce off just as quickly, as if walking past a storefront on a busy street. In most cases, this happens because they don't immediately see a way to engage with you in the future.

A landing page, also known as a lead page, can change that for you. A lead page is designed to capture your web visitors' attention, so they won't leave before engaging with your site. Most people will not buy your product or services the first time they visit your site. Usually, they ended up on your site looking for a solution to the problem they are currently facing, they checked your solution and left with a fair idea of how your solution could solve their problem. However, once they do their research, they may find other solutions or get "lost" surfing the web. If you have not found a way to keep in touch with them and to keep reminding them about what you can do for them, you are likely to be forgotten.

Your only currency at this point is to ask for their email address so that you can keep in touch. A good approach to adopt when asking people for their information is to offer something in exchange. Offering an ethical bribe in exchange for their email is an opportunity to follow up with them and offer your product, service, or promotion. An ethical bribe has the potential to work as a very strong attraction to your brand and services; hence, it is also called 'Lead Magnet.'

Let's say your visitor found you through a simple Google search or a Facebook ad. You have about 30 seconds before they decide to leave or stay. A strong lead magnet should make it a no brainer for them to leave their email with you because what they get in return will be of far higher value to them.

Example: If you sell weight-loss products, you know that your visitor is actively looking for a way to lose weight. If you were to present a way for them to do it quickly and easily without pain, it's very likely that they would be interested in what you have to say. An effective lead magnet, in this case, could be a 30-Day Challenge: "5 Ways to Lose 10 Pounds Over the Next 30 Days Without Dieting or Exercise."

The primary function of a lead capture page is to convert visitors into leads. This page works well when it is free of all distractions. Here are a few good rules to follow when designing a lead page:

- This page is designed to get web visitors to do one thing—to give you their information.
- The landing page should not provide for any navigation. This means no menu bar at the top or links to "About Us" or "Contact Us" pages.
- The only elements should be an attention-grabbing headline, a subheading expanding on the headline (e.g., Advice you won't find in any nutrition book), and an opt in box—"To find out more, enter your email address here."
- Keep it simple—The more information you ask for on this form, the less your chances of getting any information. 'Less is More' is your mantra.

Most successful businesses have one landing page for each campaign. They work best when you are launching something new, running a marketing campaign, or promoting a lead magnet, webinar, or social media campaign. A HubSpot study reveals that companies with 10 to 15 lead pages see an increase of 55% in leads. Companies with more than 40 landing pages convert at 12 times the rate of companies with 5 landing pages or less.

With this in mind, and using the guidance above, take a few minutes and plan out your landing pages

STEP 2: Let Autoresponders Take Over

Now that you have a lead and an email address, the next step is to keep up the communication at a consistent pace and manner. Relying on doing this manually is impractical, simply because it would be incredibly time-consuming. Thankfully, there's technology to our rescue. Email autoresponder software enables us to set up messages to be sent out automatically after someone subscribes to your list. An email responder can also be set up to create several messages to go out in a cycle or on a schedule.

The problem is that even when a contact subscribes to your list for a great lead magnet, usually, the most they do is read one of two pieces of content before their attention begins to taper off. They might have liked the lead magnet or promotion you offer, but at this point, you do not have a relationship with them.

To fix this, start to build a relationship by sending them emails giving them valuable content. You can also use this opportunity to introduce one of your products or services and showcase how they have helped other people with similar problems.

According to a Capterra report, every single dollar spent on email marketing resulted in about $44.25 of revenue. An autoresponder set up to effectively communicate with your subscribers not only saves time but can actually skyrocket your profits.

Most autoresponders can be configured to connect to the lead page or landing page form where you collect the email address. Setting up an autoresponder with a landing page is very easy as many software programs like ClickFunnels and Leadpages are designed to be used by non-technical users. Other options to set up autoresponders are also available free with most WordPress themes, either pre-installed or in the form of plugins.

Because the contact has subscribed to your list in exchange for a lead magnet, the first email in the cycle should be set up to deliver the lead magnet. Subsequently, the autoresponder can be set up to remind them about the reason they came to your website. This allows you to continue to build a relationship with them, going over the benefits and features of your product or service and how it can specifically solve their problem. In other words, email responders are the best tools to nurture your leads.

Take some time now to research available autoresponder software programs.

STEP 3: Nurture Your Leads

Lead nurturing is the process of engaging with individuals, who are not currently buyers but could turn into ideal customers in the future. Lead nurturing helps educate the prospect about your company, its products, and its goals—in a staggered, time-sensitive manner—in order to build trust. The goal is to build a relationship that will make it easy for the prospect to choose your offering when they are ready to make a purchase.

Nobody can expect to get married by walking up to someone and immediately proposing marriage. A relationship needs to be built over time, by getting to know their name, their interests, their personality. A carefully nurtured relationship has a high probability of getting to marriage and staying married.

In the same way, lead nurturing is rarely about pushing immediate sales. Instead, it is meant to engage the prospect through a series of marketing efforts like sending targeted content through email, digital ads, follow-ups, feedback gathering, and personalized content in order to build and maintain valuable long-term customer relationships. It's about driving real engagement and aiming for a "top of mind" recall of your brand through recurring marketing cycles.

The first step in lead nurturing is sending a welcome email. According to Entrepreneur magazine, a welcome email sent immediately after they sign up generates 320% more revenue than a promotional email and has an 86% upturn in unique open rate, along with a 196% upturn in unique click rate. Engaging a prospect immediately after signing up spikes interest but failing to do so also leads to a precipitous drop in engagement. If there was an offer of a lead magnet, it should be delivered along with the welcome mail. However, lead nurturing goes beyond the welcome email.

The second email could teach them something else—a tip or a testimonial or a success story. Maybe your own story. Or maybe a story someone else shared with you. You want to be able to pitch them to buy what you have to offer. This is a way to remind them about your offering and give them a chance to try it.

A lead nurturing sequence can consist of a link to your full sales page. At this point, it is important to remember that this sales page is not the same as the Opt-in lead page described above. This page will contain all the information your prospect needs to see in order to make a decision. Your next email could show what your offering is and showcase your differentiator from your competition. You could also show your prospects some testimonials, explain why other people found it useful, and how and why it will benefit them as well.

As discussed above, these emails should be pre-populated into your autoresponders. You don't want your newbies to forget why they are on your email list. A strategic series of emails at regular intervals can hold the interest of your prospect for a long time. A lot of people make the mistake of not following up after delivering the lead magnet and it can be a very expensive mistake.

Take some time to craft a series of emails that will nurture your prospective ideal clients into a sale.

STEP 4: Find Your Email Frequency

Now that we have established that every subscriber deserves to be nurtured through careful, frequent communication, the next question in natural order would be: how frequent is good enough?

To answer this question, I would like to refer to an example from my personal experience:

I was a regular listener of the popular National Radio show, the Howard Stern Show, for the last 25 years. The show aired at 7am every day. As the host got older, he had to scale back his days on the show to only 3 days a week. Even though I enjoyed the show just as much, I stopped tuning in as much as I used to. Why? The reason is simple, I would often forget the days his show aired. Even though I listened to his show for 25 years, I began to remember it as an afterthought because I was not following his rhythm. Then, if I happened to remember at the right time, I would go back to check if he was on. I missed most days because I fell out of sync with his frequency.

This is the main reason why email frequency is important. Email frequency is a topic that is hotly debated between experts. Too little or too much? It is always a puzzle. Most people are afraid they are going to upset their new leads if they email them too often, leading them to quickly drop off the list. But people are really busy and are receiving an overwhelming amount of emails on a daily basis. If you don't email them often, with regular intervals, they will most likely forget about you.

I have three main pieces of advice regarding email frequency:

- *Email every day.*
  The reason is simple. We are constantly in competition for space in the inbox. When people are putting their kids to bed or working in the yard, they are not exactly waiting for your email. If they only see your email infrequently, they are more likely to unsubscribe because they are less likely to relate to your rhythm.

- *If you choose to email every day, do it at the same time.*
  I get a Whole Foods email at the same time every day. If I don't get an email, I forget about them and head off to get a pizza elsewhere. Sending an email at the same time every day creates consistency, creating a rhythm for your prospect to follow. If the subscriber learns that there is no set time to expect the email, she will soon forget about it and move on to other things.

- *Write emails that 'infotain'.*

  Infotainment is a term coined for something that includes entertainment with information. A good mix is 80% entertainment and 20% tactical and practical information that leads to something you are offering or selling. Writing in a unique style that reflects your personality and using elements of storytelling are some of the most effective ways to produce emails that entertain and sell at the same time.

Consider how often your demographic would like to hear from you. How often would you like to connect with them? Make a decision and keep an eye on open rates and engagement and be ready to adjust your frequency.

STEP 5: Know Your Customers Through Segmentation

You now have your list of prospects, but can you treat them all equally? What if your list has 10 subscribers who joined today along with a bunch of people who already have signed up for your product? Quite clearly, both of them should not receive the same message from you. In this case, the new subscriber will have to be freshly nurtured towards your offering, but the person who has already signed up for your product may need to hear about an associate product(s) that will help her to further her goals.

This process where the main list is divided into further groups based on a common denominator is called List Segmentation. In the above example, the common denominator for segmenting your list is the 'stage of acquisition' of the prospects.

In the earlier weight loss program example, subscribers who are already registered to the free weight-loss challenge might be interested in seeing more information on vitamins and supplements that will aid their weight-loss journey. But new leads would be interested in knowing what the lead magnet of a 30-day workout plan contains.

A DMA study shows that segment-specific targeted messaging can increase your revenue by as much as 77%. Another MailChimp observation shows that emails sent to lists that are segmented can lead to 60% more clicks and fewer bounces and unsubscribes.

List segmentation can be divided, interpreted, and combined on a variety of criteria: Who are the people interested in your pricing? How many views of your webpage have they contributed to? Who has purchased from you? Who has downloaded the lead magnet? Who hasn't opened your emails in the last 7 days? etc.

Segmentation is possible at a very sophisticated level in order to target niche interests and products. Segmentation could be the key to your entire business because if your contact won't click on the email because it's not relevant to them, the autoresponder ranks you a bit lower. This leads to your email being sent into spam, lowering your chances of success drastically.

Consider the factors that are important for you to know and use segmentation to increase engagement.

Remember that your business begins with the relationship you build with your visitors. The entire journey can be greatly enhanced and eased with the right use of technology and a knowledge of customer acquisition principles. Effective email marketing is the foundation for your customer journey which can be your growth strategy.

More free training and resources available at: https://richlistpoorlist.com/momprenuers

Chapter 13
Keep It S.I.M.P.L.E

Natasha Mitchell
info@inspireanddrive.com

My name is Natasha Mitchell and I am a Business Strategy and Efficiency Expert. Mompreneurs hire me to help them scale their business without overwhelm, a big team, or a big budget. I'm on a mission to make business S.I.M.P.L.E so that you can make money without sacrificing your freedom.

The one thing every mompreneur needs to know when she's on the verge of burnout or considering giving up because she can't keep juggling the demands of work, clients, and family all by herself is to keep things as simple as possible in order to leverage your time, money, energy and mental bandwidth. **Here are the 5 steps to help you do that.**

STEP 1: Evaluate

As a mompreneur, you probably started your business with a vision of having more freedom and flexibility and being able to make money doing what you love, working when and where you want, and being free to spend quality time with your children and family. Right? It's the entrepreneurial dream! But it doesn't always pan out as we hoped. Why? Because most people don't take the time to consider what freedom and flexibility really means, specifically to them, personally and professionally. That's why it's necessary to evaluate what your dream life would actually look like right from the start.

When you get clear and specific on exactly what you want in life, it's easier to make decisions, prioritize projects, and decide how much time you are able to and want to spend on your business. This will help you focus your energy on what you love doing. When you let your business dictate how things need to be done, it can take over your life and drain your passion and energy. That is what ultimately takes you away from having all the fun and freedom that you really want.

I've seen so many creative and talented women give up because they can't handle the pressure any longer. This is heartbreaking because I know that the solution is very simple. When you know what to do, all it takes is a few small tweaks to turn things around and take back control of your business.

Evaluating is important because it forces you to take inventory of what is happening in your business and your life right now. When you take the time to evaluate, you are giving yourself an opportunity to decide how you want to move forward. This will help clarify your goals, which in turn helps you prioritize the ideas and projects that take you closer towards your goal and eliminate anything that takes you away from it. I suggest you ask yourself a series of questions to clarify how your business is aligned with supporting your life goals and where you may need to make adjustments. In your dream life,

- What are you doing more of?
- What are you doing less of?
- How do you serve your clients?
- How much money are you making?
- What's one thing you can change right now to help you get closer to your 'dream' life?

STEP 2: Automate

When you hear the word automation, you might immediately think technology and feel a bit intimidated. But automation doesn't have to be high tech. It can also be simply creating a checklist, routines, and repeatable processes which can also save you time and money and even improve the quality of your services.

Reflect back on Step 1, Evaluate. What is it that you want to do more of or less of in your business? Are simple tasks taking up most of your time? Are you doing a lot of work that you don't enjoy?

Time and energy are precious resources and are as important as money. When you automate simple, repetitive tasks in your business, you'll have more bandwidth for the big decisions, the profit generating work, and the work that you love; that also means having more energy for the most important people in your life—you and your family! Wondering where to start with automation? Here are a few questions to ask yourself.

- What is one task that could be automated with technology?
- What is one task that could be automated with a checklist or simple process?
- How much time per day/week would automating these tasks save you?
- What would you do with that extra time?

STEP 3: Delegate

As a working mompreneur you wear many hats. You have to juggle your kids, relationships, life obligations, and your business. This might be how you are accustomed to operating, but it is not sustainable. A lot of women get caught in the trap of feeling like they have to do everything themselves. Maybe you're a self-proclaimed control freak or perfectionist and don't think anyone can do what you do. Or maybe you're anxious about spending money. The truth is that if you want to scale your business, you can't keep doing everything and keep putting your self-care on the back burner. If you do, you and your business will suffer in the long run.

In Step 2, Delegate, I mentioned that time and energy are as valuable as money. Even when you think you are saving money by doing things yourself, there is always an opportunity cost. For example, if it takes you 5 hours to select a social media image and a freelancer can do it in 1 hour for $10, then you are valuing your time at $2 an hour. So, spending 5 hours doing something that can be quickly taken off of your plate for only $10 is a huge waste of time. You can use that time to close a new client, nurture a possible client, service an existing client, or any number of other business building activities. Or, you can choose to use that time towards self-care.

Delegating is a real mindset shift especially in the early stages of business when you are not making a lot of money. But the good news is, today there are many outsourcing sites where you can find hundreds of low-cost and capable resources. If you are not ready to invest money in delegating, you can invest time in a more productive way by bartering with someone else who has a specialty in an area you don't. And you don't have to limit yourself to only outsourcing business tasks. You can also outsource tasks around the house like cleaning, healthy meal prep, or carpooling.

To start delegating, ask yourself: What is one task you would like to delegate in business or life right now? How many hours would that save you? Considering your hourly rate, how much does it cost to do it yourself vs. outsourcing it?

STEP 4: Communicate

There comes a time in every growing business where it's time to step out of the role of employee and into the role of leader. As you step out of the day-to-day operations with automating and delegating, developing good communication skills will help you effectively lead the people supporting you.

Have you ever delegated something in the past and it didn't go exactly as planned? It's like when are guiding your children to learn something new. You've probably had to explain things several times or in several different ways at first, check in, and provide continued support. These same principles of effective communication apply to team members, clients, and vendors.

The key to successful communication and leadership is to never assume that someone knows what you are thinking; they rarely do! Be patient, give clear directions and guidance, and check-in regularly to make sure your team are following your directions as intended. The more your team works with you, understands your style and has clear processes to follow the better the results.

To make your communication more effective, write down or record the instructions. Resources such as checklists, written processes, templates, and samples are great for team members to refer to. Best communication practices include setting clear deliverables, setting clear definitions of how you measure quality and success, ensuring all parties agree upon dates and deadlines for delivery, and building in regular check-points and status updates.

Test your communication skills with this short exercise: Write down one task you want to delegate and create a step-by-step process of the key information that your team member needs to successfully complete the task.

STEP 5: Re-evaluate

The world is constantly changing and every business must continue to evolve and innovate to survive. When your business has a strong foundation and a team that supports you, you'll have more time and energy for thinking, planning, and strategizing. It is your role as the leader to keep thinking big picture and regularly monitor industry trends and changing client needs while consistently looking for ways to improve quality and performance.

As your business grows, you may have a bigger team, more clients, and more moving parts, but the #1 goal is to always keep things simple. Only do the work that you love, prioritize activities that will take you closer to your ideal life, and commit to delegating or eliminating anything that doesn't do that.

I encourage all of my clients to re-evaluate on a regular basis and you can do this by creating an annual strategy. Your strategy should be aligned to your life goals. It will guide you on your business targets, to where to prioritize your time and resources, to what you need help with, and to what investments you need to make. Your overall business strategy is an important decision-making tool that will keep you focused on what is important. It will also help you communicate your vision to your team members so they know where they are heading and how they contribute individually to the success of the business. I always recommend including your personal plans in the strategy, too. That way you will be able to see how much time you have and want to spend in your business and can ensure you build in time for your self-care, your family, and, of course, a well-deserved vacation!

If you haven't taken the time to make a plan for your business, take a few minutes to do that now. What are your financial targets for the year? What projects/services will help you achieve that? How much time does that require? How much time do you have? What help or investments do you need to make?

Your business is a bit like a child. With a good foundation, it will grow to be independent and successful and will make money without you having to supervise it every minute of the day. The key to scaling your business with ease, without a big team or a big budget, is to create a strong foundation and keep things simple.

I've created an entire business method based on keeping things S.I.M.P.L.E that will help you create a business that's totally aligned to your goals so that you can go from employee to CEO. It will guide you on how to create the repeatable systems and processes you need to be able to scale with ease, focus your energy on the work you love, and have all the time and financial freedom you desire.

Click here if you're ready for a S.I.M.P.L.E business now and I'll show you how: www.inspireanddrive.com/yes

Chapter 14

Simply Single to Genuinely Loved

Leona D. Mathews, MBA

leona@leonadmathews.com

My name is Leona Mathews and I am a Relationship Readiness Coach. I help moms recognize and attract a loving man interested in a long-term commitment, so they can stop wasting time and meet someone who is ready for love. My mission is to ready moms for a committed, loving relationship with a man who will love, encourage, support, and respect you.

The one thing every mompreneur needs to know when she's frustrated and confused because she keeps attracting the same kind of man over and over again and keeps wasting her time with the wrong guy is that she can break the never-ending cycle of dating disappointment by learning how to be selective in finding her true love. **Here are 5 steps to help you do that.**

STEP 1: Make A Dating & Relationship Plan

If you don't know where you are going, you probably won't get there. You're busy raising a family, making sure they have everything they need to thrive. You started your business with a purpose, and you have several goals in mind (financial, operational, products, sales and service). As a mompreneur, you are committed to the growth and success of your business. All that takes a boatload of time and energy which doesn't leave a lot of time for that someone special in your life. Maybe, you remember how it feels to be in love and you want to find a healthy, emotionally available man to share your life with. The problem is, you keep dating the wrong men and not finding Mr. Right. In fact, you're meeting a never-ending cycle of Mr. Wrongs. Unfortunately, you're so busy and stressed out with work and family that you wonder if you will ever find the time to get out and mingle. Let's face it, a good man is not going to automatically show up at your doorstep without an introduction. You have to be available so he can meet you. There are crises to deal with both at home and at work and tasks to complete to keep you moving toward your business goals. Your professional success has been a focal point for you, but maybe your social life is non-existent. You might be thinking to yourself, who has time to waste on men without a future? You picture him in your mind as attractive, affectionate, honest, and caring. You dream of that heartfelt connection shared by two lovers. But, somehow, you just can't make him show up in your life. To find your man without wasting precious time, you'll have to shift how you make your selection. You must consider the following in this order:

- Who he is (values such as trust and loyalty)
- What he does (common activities such as travels, enjoys sports)
- What he has (people and possessions such as children and house)

The most important part of your blueprint to success is picking a man based on the quality of his character (values), rather than his superficial traits. Can you see that focusing on "who he is" will create a strong and satisfying foundation for your relationship?

Let's get started on drafting your dating and relationship plan. Find a quiet place and some time to focus on making your plan. You may need to find a sitter for an hour or two if your kids are on the younger side. You'll want to dedicate this time to you, so put your work aside for the moment. Believe me, this is worth the time investment. Start by writing down what kind of relationship you want. That is, do you want to be married? Do you want to be in a committed relationship, but not married? Simply write it down. "I want (to be married, to be living with, to have a boyfriend…)." You get the idea. Although this seems like an easy step, I want you to really tune into your heart and follow your inner guide. Let's create your Matching Formula.

STEP 2: External (Superficial) Traits

Decide what traits are important to you in a partner (what he has and does). Normally, we have an instant impression of a man that will lead us to a "NO" or a "GO". To take it a little further, you've probably made a list of the things a marriage-minded man must have to be with you. For example, he has to have kids, own a home, have a great job, have a HOT body that turns you on, and the list continues. Whether you meet him off-line or on-line, one of the first things we do as women is to compare him to our list of his people or possessions or "what he's got." Although important, putting this as your first selection criteria won't ensure that you've got a "great guy" and it may not lead to the best match for you. For example, he may lose the material things—would that change your relationship? I call what he has and does, "superficial traits." On the other hand, a man may have a child that lives with him full time—that's a lot different than shared custody. Make a list with the title, "Have" at the top. Write down what your ideal man must have in order to create a successful relationship with you. Now, determine how your relationship would change if he no longer has these things or these things change. Write this out at the bottom of your list.

Naturally, you want to know if you have activities in common, those that you can share and enjoy with each other. Find out what he likes to do in his spare time. Do you like these same activities, or are you willing to learn? For example, he plays golf and so do you. He loves bar trivia and you do, too. He enjoys traveling and being outdoors and so do you. Common hobbies allow you opportunities to enjoy and have fun together. However, he should also be willing to learn or go to events that you love as well. Your hobbies may be tennis, golf, games and camping. Does he enjoy any of these activities?

Make a list with the title, "Do" at the top. Write down the hobbies, events, and activities you want to share with your potential partner. Put the activities you enjoy first, then the activities that you would like to do together with the expectation that these could be shared activities. The purpose of this exercise is to begin to get some clarity around how you would be spending time together.

If you are reviewing on-line dating profiles and you can tell what he likes to do, simply compare these to what you love to do. Remember, your time is precious so you don't want to spend extra time with someone that you will not enjoy. Again, "superficial traits" are important in the full scheme of selection, but not at the top.

STEP 3: The Quality of His Character

This is the essential step to finding a relationship that will last a lifetime. Selecting your partner based on the quality of his character (values) and ensuring that his values match yours, will create the strongest foundation for your healthy, loving relationship. Your values are about being who you are, what you stand for and how you live your life. They are often driven by your beliefs and behaviors. The quality of his character or his values are the first place you want to look when making the decision to date him and whether he has relationship potential. When you are comfortable, happy and in sync with each other, that's a match. Make a list with the title, "Values" at the top. Write down 5 or more of your core values. Be honest with yourself. For example, if you say you value reliability, are you showing up as a reliable person? That is, are your actions congruent with your words? If not, you may need to do some growing in this area. Of course, you don't have to have the same exact values as he does, but the more similarities, the better. Do you see how this eliminates a number of candidates and saves you time and frustration? Additionally, it opens up time and space for the men who are going to be your best match. I know you want to be with someone special. What makes him special is that he is compatible with you in the most important areas of a relationship.

STEP 4: Love And Relationship Boundaries

When you are clear about what you want and what's most important to you for that match made in heaven, create some guidelines around who you will and will not date. This will save you heartache!

This requires saying YES to those who are a great fit and NO to those that will never make you happy. Read his profile if you are dating online. If you are offline, have conversations about his values, hobbies, and history. After you find out more about him, you can decide if you are likely to make a loving connection. Here is an example of how the comparison works. You want to be married and he doesn't, eliminate him; he's not what you are looking for. If your values are not in sync with his, don't date him. If you have no activities in common (he likes ice fishing and you like sunbathing) and the two of you can't agree on finding activities together, don't date him. Extra tip for those who are online: If he doesn't have a picture or fill out the profile, immediately pass on him. He's shopping and not ready for a serious relationship. This may seem harsh, but your time is precious, and you don't want to waste your energy on someone that isn't going to fulfill your most precious desire. Go back and look at your list. Make sure that you are sorting and selecting men based on the above guidelines, in this order:

- Quality of Character (values such as honesty and loyalty)
- Common Activities (what he likes to do such as travel and family get togethers)
- People and Possessions (what he has such as family and home....)

STEP 5: Boost Your Confidence

When you are confident, it's easier to set boundaries based on your guidelines. You'll be able to date with poise, share how you feel, and ask for what you want. The more relaxed you feel, the more you will enjoy the time you spend with each other. Being able to say NO, when it is not a great fit, will stop you from wasting time. This also helps you feel self-assured, so you know when you are dating Mr. Right for the right reasons.

Follow these simple tips to start building confidence in yourself. Stop the negative self-talk. When you are telling yourself things like, "I'm not attractive enough to have a man in my life," or, "I'm so dumb; who would want to be with me?", you're blocking the energy and vibration that you need to attract a healthy man. Why? Because like attracts like. Instead, turn your talk around. For example, tell yourself, "Men find me attractive," or, "I'm a life-long learner and happy to share what I know,"

No more comparing yourself to others. Comparisons create self-judgment and we can be overly critical of ourselves. You'll never be what someone else is, nor should you want to be. Accept yourself as a unique and beautiful woman who adds her own spark to this life.

You don't have to be perfect; just be the best version of yourself. Trying to be perfect is unrealistic. As women, we see so many advertisements showing the perfect body, stunning personality and financial success. Being true to yourself and showing up as who you are is better than competing to be the "perfect" woman.

Here is the best way to immediately build your confidence and trust in yourself:

Say what you are going to do, do what you said you would do, and acknowledge that you did it. Acknowledging yourself for walking your talk reinforces the reliability factor. You know you will follow through and therefore, will build your trust in yourself. Let's review the steps to recognizing and being ready for the type of relationship you want:

1. Make a dating and relationship plan.
2. Know and embrace the traits in a man that are important to you.
3. Recognize the qualities you want and need in a man who is ready for a committed relationship.
4. Set your boundaries based on your Matching Formula.
5. Build your confidence so you can easily say YES to the men who are a great fit and NO to those that are not a match.

Use the steps above to stop wasting your time with the wrong men and start finding your very own true love! As a Relationship Readiness Expert, I want to help you quickly sort through the potentials and find Mr. Right so you can have the love you deserve and desire.

Schedule a complimentary call with me to see if I'm the right person to help you find your match made in heaven: http://bit.ly/talktoleona

Chapter 15

Achieve Your Business Goals

Sarah Olivieri

sarah@pivotground.com

My name is Sarah Olivieri. I'm a Business Strategist and Creator of the Impact Method™. I help mompreneurs facing burnout get focused so they can stop wasting their time and energy on things that don't really move the needle forward and finally be able to have the business and life they've always wanted. My mission is to help heart-driven mompreneurs take one great next step after another so they can thrive.

The one thing every mompreneur needs to know when she's feeling burnt out, stuck, or overwhelmed with her business, is that the secret to getting unstuck and regaining yourself, your sanity, and your time is to have a great strategy (aka "plan") that meets you where you are and helps you pivot to where you want to go, and the secret to a great strategy is setting better goals. **Here are 5 steps to help you do that.**

STEP 1: Maximize Your Mission

Your mission is your ultimate destination, the place all your goals are taking you to, at least, as best as you can define it right now. Some people seem to be born with a dream and, if you're one of those people, you'll know exactly what your mission is. But this isn't true for everyone, and, for those of you, I want to tell you that it's OK to not know what your dream is; you can still have a mission. The reason that having a clear and specific mission adds value to setting great goals and having an incredible strategy is that it helps you stay focused. It also helps other people who are going to help you in your business be aligned with your journey. In other words, having a well-defined mission gives you momentum, and nothing makes achieving goals more rewarding than achieving them quickly! Sure, you can skip ahead to Step 2 and start setting any goal, but if you really want to maximize your results, it's important to know your mission and only set goals that help you get there. If you have a ton of goals that don't help you achieve your mission, you either need to adjust your mission or have a real heart-to-heart with yourself about letting go of your goals that aren't moving the needle forward toward your mission because spending time and energy on those goals are likely holding you back from success.

To help you crystallize your mission, take it out of your head and write it down. Try to be as specific as possible and don't forget to give yourself permission to dream big and to dive into enough specifics to make your mission unique to you. If you're having trouble, try this: Create three columns. In the first column, write down who will be impacted by your mission. Is it just you? Is it about your whole family? Is it your business? Is it a segment of the population? In column 2, write down *how* those people will be affected or impacted. This could be something that the people in column 1 are doing, a new state of being, or something they have learned or achieved. Finally, the 3rd column addresses the how question. In the 3rd column, write down any constraints or specific requirements around the way in which the impact will occur. If you aren't a wordsmith, you can leave these three columns as your mission, or, if you are so inclined, go ahead and rewrite the content of the three columns into one or two catchy sentences that will be your mission. Here is an example from my own life.

- Column 1, *Who*: me and my son
- Column 2, *What* (Impact): have a business that is fulfilling, son attending private school, and have a comfortable life
- Column 3, *How* (Requirements): $120,000 personal income from my business without working more than 28/hours per week

STEP 2: Get Clear On Outcomes
One of the biggest realizations for me in setting better goals was understanding that there are actually two types of goals that work together to get us what we want. The first type of goal that you need to set is an outcome. Outcomes are

results that we don't actually have control over; however, they are, hopefully, the results of well-planned actions. In fact, your mission is an outcome goal. We naturally tend to put ourselves at the center of our own stories and this causes us to phrase outcomes as though they are in our control. For example, I bet at one point, maybe even now, you have the goal to "make more money " Unless you are the Treasury, though, the outcome you are really thinking about is getting other people to hand their money over to you. Once we separate the outcomes from the direct actions we can take, we can start to set truly great goals.

Now, let's go a little deeper in our understanding of outcomes. I break the category of outcome goals into two subtypes. First is what I like to call an Impact Goal. This is something that you want to have happen which is somehow physical in nature. It can be a new state of being, a possession, or an action that you want someone else to take. The second type I like to call a Perception Goal. A Perception Goal is when the outcome represents a change in the way someone thinks or feels. Often, but not always, when we set an Impact Goal, we realize that we need to achieve a Perception Goal first in order to have a chance at the desired impact. For example, if I want people to buy my product (Impact Goal), I first need them to believe that my product will solve a problem for them (Perception Goal). In other words, it's often the case that in order to change the way someone acts, you first have to change the way they think or feel. Whenever you find that you've identified a Perception Goal, you have a big clue about the kinds of actions you can take. Can you guess what they are? They will probably be actions related to marketing or branding. Take a moment to think about your mission and define one to three outcome goals that would need to happen in order to get you closer to achieving your mission. Label each outcome goal as either an Impact Goal or Perception Goal.

STEP 3: Get Hyper Specific About What You Can Do

Now that you know what the outcome is that you're trying to achieve, it's time to get hyper specific about what actions are within your control that are likely to have the desired outcome. I call these Execution Goals because they are within your direct control to execute. For example, if you want people to believe that your product will solve their problem (Perception Goal), you may want to take an action related to marketing (Execution Goal). Or, if you want your business to run without you (Impact Goal), you may want to hire a team member (Execution Goal). Your Execution Goal is not a task, it's the sum or the end point of several tasks. These goals should be written in a way the provides measurable outcomes, so everybody knows when and if the Execution Goal has been completed. Let's say you want 10 existing clients to buy your new product (Impact Goal), here are some examples of corresponding Execution Goals.

• Call all my existing clients and tell them about the new product.
• Send out a 3-part email series to my list explaining the value of the new product with a call to action to buy it.

For those of you familiar with SMART goals, you might be wondering if your goals need to be "time bound." What I've found is that all goals naturally have timelines that are unique to them. If your outcome goals have a time by which they need to be accomplished in order to be relevant, then all the subsequent Execution Goals should be time bound, too. If your outcomes don't have a timeline, your Execution Goals may naturally have one. For example, you may have a marketing related Execution Goal that involves taking advantage of the holiday season. This would obviously become irrelevant if you didn't get it done by the holidays. If your Execution Goals don't have a timeline, then we'll get to timing in Step 4. Now, go back to your notes and for each outcome goal you've written, try writing down at least one Execution Goal.

STEP 4: Build Your Action Plan

Your goals and your strategy are only as good as your ability to execute them and that's why you should create a written plan of action for each Execution Goal. What you'll need to do is define specific and manageable action steps. I call these Action Sets, because they are a set of steps or to-dos that you will need to do in order to achieve your Execution Goal. Each Execution Goal will have at least one Action Set and each Action Set will have one or more to-do items in it. Actions sets should be time bound, even if the goals they support aren't. My general rule of thumb is that you should be able to complete an Action Set within a two-week period. If you have an Action Set that will take much longer, try breaking it down into multiple Action Sets. Here is an example: if your Execution Goal is to hire a new team member, you might have the following action sets (each with a list of to-dos).

- Define the job.
- Advertise the position.
- Interview and select a candidate.
- Onboard your new hire.

Now it's time to go back to your notes and for each execution goal write the title(s) of the Action Sets that you will need to do in order to achieve that Execution Goal.

STEP 5: Rinse And Repeat

Setting goals is an imperfect process even once you've mastered the formula above. The reason is that we don't know what we don't know at the time we set them. Even when I've set amazingly "clear" goals, there's nothing like 20/20 hindsight to make me realize I missed an important detail. But not to worry! There is a way to fix the hindsight problem. All you have to do is frequently return to your goals and update them. I recommend doing a mini check of your Action Sets every two weeks and a thorough check of all your goals every two months. Make a practice of setting aside a little time on your calendar every 2 weeks for this mini-check and a longer time (about 1 hour) to do a deep-dive review of all your goals once every two months. Go ahead and block the time out on your calendar now.

For years, my life and business were full of false starts and left me overwhelmed and frustrated because I was terrible at setting goals. One day, I decided I was going to master goals once and for all. My life literally depended on it. I was leaving an unhappy marriage, beyond broke, and was a newly single mom of a 3-year-old boy. Before long I had the business I wanted and the life I wanted for me and my son—working less than 28 hours a week and, best of all, I stopped working on Fridays. Now I'm humbled to be able to share with you the same goal setting framework that allowed me to pivot and thrive.

I believe that no matter how stuck you feel, there is always a better way that begins with one simple and great next step. I have a great next step for you!

Download my goal setting templates at: www.pivotground.com/mom-goals

Chapter 16

Embrace Your Entrepreneurial Goddess

Fay Skandsen

Fay@FayHouse.no

My name is Fay Skandsen. I am a Self-Empowerment Goddess and I help mompreneurs wake up to their true potential so you can stop with all of the negativity and self doubt and finally be able to shine your light into the world and serve all the people you are meant to help with your amazing work. My mission is to enlighten mompreneurs to their inner power to help them achieve success.

The one thing every mompreneur needs to know when she's struggling with her confidence is that she can discover her personal power by connecting with herself. **Here are 5 steps to help you do that.**

STEP 1: Understand The Power Of Beauty

Beauty is as powerful as Truth and Love—in my opinion, they're two of the most powerful things in the world! Beauty is a quality in a person that gives pleasure to the senses and exalts the mind and spirit.

However, when women hear or think about the word "beauty," it is often so charged with the wrong emotions. Unfortunately, as small girls, we are continuously measured and valued by our outer beauty. We begin to think about the word as an expression of what we look like and measure ourselves and others towards our idea of what beauty looks like. This can be catastrophic to our healthy development and our well-being.

There is an entire industry designed specifically to thrive on women's self-doubt and self-criticism. We are led to believe that we need to do things differently from what is natural to us, to be something we are not, or to add or subtract something from the way we look in order to be truly beautiful.

You were born beautiful. Your beauty comes from within.

When working with my clients, I guide them to think about beauty in an expansive way and teach them how beauty can be found everywhere. Think about the beauty in a smile, in a sunset, in a landscape, or in a clean and productive workspace. Beauty is indeed everywhere. However, the true power of beauty resides inside each and every one of us—our inner beauty.

When you begin to understand the power of real beauty and start seeing it everywhere, not just on the outside in the external world, but also within you— you will connect with your inner self in such a different way.

When you find that spiritual connection to yourself, you will feel content, filled with love, and have a sense of complete wellness. When connected to your inner beauty, you are in such a wonderful place. This may be one of the few times that you crave nothing and are completely satisfied.

Think about the last time you watched a beautiful sunset. Did you, at any time, feel the desire for it to be something different? No. You watched in awe and let the beauty of that sunset fill you. How about when you look inside yourself? Do you feel the same way? Do you view yourself with awe and a feeling of goodness?

As a woman, there is a part of you that is wired to connect to beauty. Imagine what could happen for you when you open up to your inner power and you connect to your love of beauty. Whether you believe you are beautiful or not, whether you have been told that you are beautiful or not, is completely irrelevant. You are undeniably beautiful as there is beauty everywhere. You are beautiful inside and out. Your beauty comes from within and cannot help but shine out.

You were born with special gifts, and the most precious of them all is the beauty of being YOU. You have something to give to this world that nobody else can give. Your inner force is already fueled by this feeling and is ready for you when you are ready to open up to it.

This is your source of power and society has gone to extremes to stop you from connecting to this inner source! It's of utmost importance that you connect to your inner power because without this strong connection, it will be hard for you to be powerful and impact the people you are meant to make a difference for.

You may not be able to accomplish this overnight, but you can start working toward it today. When clients first come to me, I show them through several exercises how to help them realize their inner beauty.

You can try to open your heart and feel the love you have within you right now. Find a quiet space where you can sit or lie down. Become very still and listen for any words that arise from deep inside of you. Say this affirmation with your silent inner voice. You can do this any time during the day or whenever you need to calm down and just find inner peace.

"I'm truly beautiful. I have a gift and I will show my gratitude by sharing my gift with the world. I am proud of who I am and connect with my inner source. I awaken my true Goddess to empower me in my daily work. She keeps me connected to my heart so that I stay in alignment with the work I am called to do on this planet.

Reject any negative thoughts as you connect with your inner source and know that when you embrace your inner beauty you will feel whole and completely accepted.

Make it a daily practice to have decluttered, immaculate, and beautiful surroundings. Make sure to clean your workspace every day. Have fresh flowers and throw away garbage. Enjoy the beauty inside of you and enjoy the beauty around you.

STEP 2: Understand Your Power

Do you ever stop to think about what being a woman really means? As mompreneurs, we are so busy with our kids, our partners, our businesses, our extended families, our responsibilities, and all this busy-ness can make us forget how amazing and powerful we really are. The fact that we can do so much for so many people is, in itself, amazing!

What is most amazing, though, is that we are the only ones who can carry another life inside of us. Whether we actually give birth or not, is beyond my point right now. Being able to carry and give birth to new life makes us true Goddesses. Throughout evolution, we women keep humanity alive. This is possible because we are so incredibly powerful. You have heard the joke, haven't you? The one that "if it were up to men to give birth, civilization would end." This is no joke. It takes a certain strength and endurance to give birth and raise children. This strength is tied to female power.

Knowing our worth and inner power is tied to our identity. Too many women don't actually know who they are. Identifying your true self is one of the most powerful discoveries you will have in life. When you know who you are and stand in your power, you will naturally define what you allow into your life. Your boundaries become clear. You stop people from pushing you around and you embrace your own strength.

You will feel a fierce pride. The beautiful thing about this is that it will penetrate all areas of your life. Everyone will take notice and will treat you differently as you begin to treat yourself differently. Remember that a powerful, strong woman doesn't mean that you need to be angry or yelling or loud. Many strong women have a very quiet strength. Each mompreneur shows her strength in her own unique way.

The following is an exercise I use with my clients to help motivate them to develop their inner power and strength:

Take some time to consider how different your life and business will be if you are deeply aware of and intentionally stand in your power. In this exercise, I'll focus on business prompts, but of course, you would apply this to all areas of your life.

- How would your work change?
- Would you charge more for your work?
- Would you be more selective of your clients?
- Would you have more clients?
- Would you be more confident in your work?
- Would you be happier in your work?

STEP 3: Understand The Power Of Speaking And Acting Truthfully

As women, we are taught from a very young age to "keep the peace" and make sure everybody gets along. One part of this is to act as if we agree, even when we don't, and then try to justify it to feel better about it. This can be dangerous for us because it oppresses our honest feelings. Deep down inside we know the truth. So why do we go against how we think and feel? Because we don't feel worthy enough or are afraid of rejection. We are worthy enough, though, and if the relationship cannot withstand the dissonance, is it worthy? Your thoughts, your words, your actions, all have an energetic component, and when they are not in alignment with who you are, you are hurting yourself on an energetic level. You are lying to yourself and to others. And, on a certain level, you must know that there are consequences to lying.

When you begin to wake up your Inner Goddess, you will have to be more truthful. But don't worry, being truthful doesn't mean that you need to be nasty or rude. There are many ways to tell the truth. You can be kind and empathetic and still stand in your power. For example, previously, when a client asked you to do something that you were not comfortable with, you may have impulsively come up with a small lie in order to feel comfortable saying "no." Many women feel compelled to give a reason why they are saying "no." When you connect with your Entrepreneurial Goddess, you will realize that you do not owe anyone an explanation as to why you say no.

It is often in the explanation, that the lie is given. One way to handle this is to say, "no, I won't do that, as it doesn't resonate with me." Practice saying what it is you need to say in an honest and direct way. Even the little lies hurt. People know they are being lied to and you know that you are lying. Make a commitment to yourself that you will stop lying. Practice truthfulness in everything you do, including social media. This will make you stand out as a strong and powerful woman. Think of Frida Kahlo or Madonna or Pink—

they all made their mark by being truthful about who they are and what they stand for.

Feeling confident enough to be completely honest is so empowering. When you practice truthfulness, you understand how powerful it is when empowered people speak their truth and take a stand for their beliefs, not just for you and for your clients, but also for our planet.

When you are ready, let your clients know that you have made this commitment to yourself. Write an email letting your followers know that you love what you do, and that your biggest intention for your business is to align with the Universe and be as truthful as possible. My clients tell me that this is one of their favorite exercises as their work and the relationships with their clients become deeper and more meaningful.

STEP 4: Spread The Positivity

Everything you think, speak, and do has a certain kind of energy, and this energy radiates out into the world. It is contagious, so make sure that what you send out is something you want to give away. When you feel good about who you are, you show up with confidence. By thinking good thoughts, acting positively, and speaking with compassion, you will love who you are and show up accordingly. When you do, you connect with The Goddess in you and feel an inner alignment. The beautiful thing about being in alignment is that everything just makes sense.

I know that as mompreneurs, we have way more on our plate than most people. It can be hard to always be mindful of everything we say and do. However, when you commit to connecting with your Goddess, you will see that it becomes much easier to speak, act, and think positively. When you think about your Inner Goddess, you can't help but smile, right? Your Goddess is made of pure goodness, light, and love. The more you are in alignment with her, the easier it will be for you to spread positivity.

One way I encourage my clients to spread positivity is to find at least one thing every day to highlight and talk about in a positive way. We call it "today's positive news." Too much news these days is bad news, but you can bring positive news to your tribe! Brag about yourself or your clients. Talk about other peoples' accomplishments and praise their progress. This will make you feel great and it will make them feel awesome. Your clients will appreciate being acknowledged and valued. When you think, talk, and act positively all the time, more amazing things will happen for you.

To infuse your everyday with power, begin a practice of spreading positivity every day.

STEP 5: Understand The Power Of Sisterhood

As a mompreneur, you understand exactly what other mompreneurs have gone through and are going through. Every woman is your sister, of course. As a mompreneur, your path is even more aligned. Women go through so much. We carry the burden and the weight of all the people we love. We are often holding the pain, shame, loneliness, and despair of others as we manage all of our complex feelings. We are responsible for our families, our partners, our communities and ourselves. Being a mompreneur just adds a whole new layer to it all.

Most of us have not been honored as the true Goddesses that we are. We are taught that life is a competition and both in business and life, women are competing against each other. We are all sisters on the same path, though. When we see this and acknowledge our sameness and that we are all on this journey together, we recognize the incredible power that sisterhood holds. There is no competition. When we recognize this common path, competing feels impossible and useless.

In business, it's possible that someone else may be chosen over you, but this has got nothing to do with competition—this is a matter of preference. This perspective is important, because competition is by nature divisive. When we stand together, we are so much stronger. As a tribe of Goddesses, we are unstoppable! By letting go of destructive ideas that have been thrust upon us since we were girls and adopting a more loving and expansive view of how we should be thinking about and treating one another, we empower ourselves and each other.

What you can do today to step into this beautiful way of thinking and being is to take a stand for us all being on the same side. Reach out to another mompreneur in the same area of work that you do and ask if she would be open to working together to support each other in a deeper way. When you know of another mompreneur experiencing a challenge, give them a shoulder to cry on, time to vent, or offer advice. Reach out to a sister in a loving way. Call her and tell her how much you admire her or write a beautiful recommendation on her page so that she feels and sees your support. Just knowing that you care can lift another sister.

Know that you are a Goddess with the innate power to change everything around you. Use this knowledge to change everything around you for the better. This will make you a powerful sister surrounded by supportive women and will grow your sisterhood of Goddesses all around the world.

If you are ready to connect with your strength and power and meet your Goddess, please visit my website to learn more: www.fayskandsen.com

Chapter 17
Eradicate Imposter Syndrome

Jasmin Tak Shum
Support@TheGreatThingsInLife.com

My name is Jasmin Tak Shum and I am a Confidence and Clarity Coach. I help mompreneurs understand their value and build their confidence so they can stand in their authentic power and charge what they are worth. My mission is to empower mompreneurs to shine their light and make the money that they deserve.

The one thing every mompreneur needs to know when she's working way too hard for way too little money, is that she needs to recognize her own value first, in order for others to be able to see the value in her. **Here are 5 steps to help you do that.**

STEP 1: Know The 2-Step Rule

Many coaches and mentors are afraid to charge what they are worth because they mistakenly believe that they need to know everything on the planet on their topic. Are you one of them? I know I used to be.

The truth is, it's just not possible for you to know everything and nobody expects you to. None of us possess all of the information from the entire universe—not even Google knows everything. Don't you learn something new every day? I know I do! This is what keeps our lives interesting, the fact that we are always learning and discovering.

In this day and age, there is almost too much information available that we have easy and instant access to. It's not just books, podcasts and experts anymore.

We live in a time of "information overload" to the point that we can no longer decide quickly what is right or beneficial for us anymore. So often, we become paralyzed because there is just so much content for us to consume; we don't even know where to start! What this means is that your clients aren't really looking for more information. They are looking for curated information. They are looking for someone to take all of the information that is paralyzing them and to put it together in a condensed way that is easy to understand. They are looking for support. They are looking for help with implementation. They are looking for someone who has experience with what challenges them. They are looking for feedback. They want to resonate with someone so that they can make decisions that feel aligned with their wants and desires. They are looking for a whole lot of things that do not include all the information in the universe.

Therefore, your ideal prospective clients are not just paying for your information, but more so, they are paying for your support and for your knowledge disseminated in a way that resonates with them. In other words, it's not so much about the "what," as much as it is about the "how" that they are attracted to. We all have different learning styles and capabilities and are drawn to different teachers.

This brings me to "The 2-Step Rule." Essentially, we only need to be 2 steps ahead of our clients; you just need to know a bit more than they do in order to help them. There are many stages in a client's journey, my guidance is to focus on helping the ones that are 2 steps behind you so that as you grow your knowledge, you will be able to support them as they move to their next stage.

For example, many years ago, I felt very lost in my life and was looking for clarity. There was a coach that I had been following for a few years and a part of me was desperate for her guidance. However, I felt intimidated by her decades of experience and felt that she wouldn't understand where I was because the "gap" between us was just too wide. I was a newbie on my self-discovery journey and felt very "small," due to my lack of confidence, and didn't feel comfortable being in her presence. Because of this, I was more drawn to the coaches that could relate to my experience at that moment (the ones that were just 2 steps ahead of me). So, although I was following a coach with much more knowledge, I hired the one that I was more comfortable with because her own experience felt more aligned with where I was in my own development. Here are 2 prompts that can help you see that your knowledge is enough and valuable.

- Think of 3 situations where you were able to solve your potential clients' challenges. How were you able to give them the outcome they needed or wanted?
- How did your solving their challenge help them?

STEP 2: Know That You Do Not Need To Fit Into A Box

We often feel like we have to be like our gurus in order to be a successful entrepreneur. But it's important to understand that we are all different and that "no two snowflakes are the same." We do not need to be the same as others when it comes to business or even our private life. Yes, there might be certain techniques that you would want to learn and practice and develop; however, the important part is for you to be completely aligned with who you are because your ideal clients will be attracted to you and your authenticity.

It might take a while for you to build up your business, but please do not give up. It is extremely common for new entrepreneurs to feel like they are treading water and their work is not getting noticed or being appreciated. Creating a successful business takes time. It takes time for your tribe to find you, so be sure to create content and visibility opportunities whenever you can. Create a schedule for yourself and stick to it.

One of my clients was so lost in her coaching business. She had spent so much time and money following an "expert" in her field and trying to copy everything he did so that she could be as successful. The problem was, she didn't really know what he had sacrificed in life to become successful. We are only able to copy what we see. So many factors go into being successful, but all she was able to see was what the expert was willing to show her! And, of course, she is a completely different snowflake! So, she has different dreams and desires than the expert does. For example, the expert was a single man without children. He traveled often and had all the time in the world to work on his business. For all we know, it's possible he was a workaholic! On the other hand, my client was a devoted mom. She did not have the time or the interest in investing that amount of energy into her business. She was trying to follow a roadmap that led to a destination she didn't want to reach. She did not want to be a workaholic! And this is the problem with trying to fit into somebody else's box. Trying to listen to so many different voices and trying to copy what somebody else is doing can be like poison to your soul. I suggested that she take inventory on what makes her special and what she wants to get out of her business. I showed her how important it was to be really intentional about what it is that you want for yourself. This is not about copying anyone else because you cannot copy a person. This is about being clear about who you are and what you want. When we copy other people, it's because we aren't clear about who we are and what we want. We mistakenly believe that other people know better and we don't believe that we will achieve our own success unless we copy their path. But each person's path is uniquely theirs. And trying to be something you're not is not sustainable. Instead, consider deciding what your own path should be and take steps towards your goals.

My guidance would be to look for patterns in the "experts" and programs that you feel drawn to copy or blindly follow. What is it about them that you find so compelling? What is it that you would like to have? The purpose of this exercise is to have you discern what part of the fantasy you actually want. Through this exercise, my client was able to recognize that it wasn't the expert's life that she wanted. Actually, she thought he was lonely and too fanatical in his business. Together, we were able to tease out that what she really wanted was the freedom his business provided which allowed him to travel at a moment's notice. Knowing this gave her the clarity she needed to decide to create a business plan that allowed for more of a freedom-filled lifestyle. Figuring out exactly why you are attracted to these people and programs will help you define what it is you really want.

The second part of this is to focus on what you love about yourself so that you are spending more time looking inward instead of outward. What are the traits and characteristics that you absolutely love about yourself? Create a daily self-appreciation routine where you express gratitude towards yourself, your body parts, your compassion, your humor, your taste, your quirkiness, your honesty, etc.

STEP 3: Acknowledge Who You Are

Often, we don't fully know who we are at a conscious level. I am not talking about whether you are a mother, a daughter, a grandmother, a wife, a sister, or a business owner, etc. I am referring to who we are deep down without all the external identities. So many mompreneurs suffer from imposter syndrome because they are so busy being what somebody else wants them to be that they forget who they really are. Many women spend their whole lives trying to please others.

Why do we do this to ourselves? It's a terrible thing to feel that you need to be someone other than who you are to please others. This has to stop in order for you to re-discover your value. You are a very special and unique human being that is worthy and deserving. You may not feel that at this very moment, but it's important to begin to move towards that feeling. And the first step in moving towards that feeling is being able to understand yourself because the more that we understand ourselves, the stronger our foundation becomes. When we know who we are, we can make decisions with confidence based on what is truly important to us—regardless of what other people want for us or think we should want. We need to truly know ourselves inside and out so that we can take a stand for what serves us and easily say no to what is not desirable.

Tune in to yourself to understand what makes you unique, what your skill sets are, what your desires are, and what is important to you. Ask yourself a number of black and white questions. This will help you to determine where you land. You will find that you are not always in one camp or the other. For some questions, you will land in the gray area. This is all important information! It will lead you to a real picture of what makes you the special person that you are. And when you know who you are, you can make decisions that are in alignment with who you are.

Some examples of black or white questions:
- Are you a morning person or a night person?
- Are you a spontaneous person or do you like predictability?
- Are you outgoing or a homebody?

Now ask yourself a series of interest questions:
- Do you like sports, dancing or singing?
- Do you like fine dining, prefer fast food, or a home-cooked meal?
- What kind of movies do you prefer?

Lastly, ask yourself:
- What are you core values?

Knowing your core values is important because when we surround ourselves with people that are not in alignment with our core values, it can be extremely uncomfortable.

STEP 4: Accept And Forgive Yourself

Self-Acceptance is more than just a verbal statement that you just blurt out. It is a deep, deep consent and approval of ourselves, our behavior, our thought process, our preferences etc. This doesn't mean that there isn't anything undesirable or that we don't love about ourselves. It's that we have made the decision to come to terms with and be completely at peace with those particular parts of ourselves or circumstances. It's that we accept ourselves fully. When we do not fully accept ourselves, we are, in essence, rejecting ourselves. Therefore, in order to accept ourselves unconditionally, we must stop rejecting parts of ourselves.

Rejecting ourselves is like having a civil war within us. Do you think we can be mentally, emotionally, and physically healthy and harmonious when we are constantly at war with ourselves? Of course not.

Maybe you are upset with yourself that you haven't been charging your worth. Or maybe you haven't been charging at all. You might be beating yourself up and hating the part of you that won't stand up for yourself. But being mad, angry, and blaming ourselves for not doing something in the past isn't helpful. Now that you know that you have enough knowledge and know your value, you can make a commitment to yourself to communicate your worth to your prospective clients and only work when getting paid your value. Forgiving your earlier mistakes and wholly accepting yourself will allow you to move forward with your life in a healthy and productive way so you can stop living in your past.

Accepting yourself is a key step in eradicating imposter syndrome. Let's wipe our chalkboard clean so that we can start anew.

Try this exercise:

When you need to forgive and accept yourself, take a moment and repeat the following statement:

"I forgive myself completely and unconditionally. I'm grateful that I am in the process of (what you are turning around, in this case, charging your worth)."

Repeat this mantra every day for a month and see the difference it creates.

STEP 5: Bask In Your Worthiness

You are not the only person who works in your area of expertise. However, you are the ONLY person that brings together your unique experience that is a culmination of all the lessons that you have learned and all the information you have gathered. You are the ONLY person that can provide the impact that you provide in JUST the way that you do. No other person on the planet can do it the same way.

Therefore, it stands to reason, that if you do NOT provide your service, in a way that only you can do it, all of those people out there that would have been impacted by you would be left suffering! Can you see how important your work is? If you do not charge for your work OR do not charge your worth, eventually you will not be able to continue providing your amazing service. Many coaches are forced to quit their coaching service and get a job because they are unable to pay their bills. Can you imagine what a great loss that would be to all of the people out there who desperately need what you have to offer?

It's important for you to understand the value that you provide to your clients as well as the impact that you make in their lives. Without knowing the value that you bring to the table, you won't be able to stand behind the investment that you will charge. This is a primary reason why many coaches work for free, discount their offerings or feel guilty getting paid.

For example, as a Confidence and Clarity Coach, when I am able to help you be a more confident person, then you are able to charge your worth which will create financial freedom for you. But how else does my work impact my client's lives? When my clients make more money, they can work less, which could mean more free time for you and your family. When my clients make more money, it could mean that their children can go to college. Financial freedom could save a marriage burdened by financial stress.

When you begin to think of your work in this way, can you see how many different ways your work is valuable?

Take some time now to define all the different ways your work will impact your client, your client's life and the people in her life. There may be 10 different ways that your client will benefit as a result of working with you. As you look over all of the incredible value that you provide and the remarkable impact your work has had or will have on so many lives, marvel at the huge difference you are making. I would like you to consider that without your work, your ideal client will continue to suffer. This should help you see your value for what it is— invaluable!

Imposter Syndrome is something that can be easily eradicated when you understand the value that you are providing and the impact that you are making with your work. Following these steps will help you realize that you are worthy of being paid well.

If you would like to learn more about how I can help you acknowledge, accept, and embrace your true value so that you can stop settling for crumbs and start owning your worth, please visit www.FacingImposterSyndrome.com

Chapter 18

Boundary Setting for Success

Susan Nelson

snelson@pragmatic-life.com

My name is Susan Nelson. I am a Career Coach and Leadership Advisor and I help you win at the work-life tug of war so you can go from feeling minimized and underappreciated to thriving as a mompreneur! My mission is to help mompreneurs be indispensable to both their business and their families by helping them successfully discover their voice, own their power, and increase their overall impact both in business and at home.

The one thing every mompreneur needs to know when she's feeling minimized or underappreciated by clients or her family in her dual role as both a business owner and a mom is that establishing healthy boundaries will give her long-term success. **Here are 5 steps to help you do that.**

STEP 1: Check In With Yourself—Where Is Your Heart At?

I know, I know what you're thinking—it sounds a bit fluffy, but really, you're better able to serve when you are clear on what fills your bucket and lights you up! And that starts with your heart.

The idea is to tackle this preemptively, so that when the moment strikes, you are prepared. So, take a moment now to slow down a bit and check in with yourself—what's most important to you? How do you want to feel? Is it time to slow down and take some time for yourself to rejuvenate? Do you need to be more present with someone in the family who may be struggling and need your help? Is it time to get laser focused and ramp up your business? Where are your life's needs at this moment in time?

Once you know what it is you want and how you want to feel, this becomes your compass, your 'true north' that will make day-to-day decisions so much easier! Trust me, taking this time to check in will illuminate your priorities like a neon sign and make you super clear on what to say 'YES' to and, more importantly, what to say 'NO' to.

As with seasons, our priorities and desired feelings can shift over time, so it's important to regularly check in with yourself to see where you are at. For some of my clients who are in the midst of raising younger children, it may be important for them to limit their work hours and only consider business opportunities that fit within a part-time schedule. This way, they can have the breathing room they need to take better care of themselves and be more present for their families. Others may have more time to invest in their businesses and may be focused on expanding or shifting to work that really lights them up.

Three questions to ask yourself today:
- What is most important to me at this stage in my life?
- How do I want to feel?
- What will help me feel this way more often?

These will help reveal your path, guide your decision making, and are the beginning of establishing a healthy boundary practice that will allow you to feel more of what you want to feel without the guilt!

STEP 2: Watch Out For Time-Sucks

You know what I mean, those things that sneak into your schedule and, before you know it, they hijack your whole day or even week. Maybe you can identify with this: You've got 2-3 tasks that you need to get done today, and you've even blocked out adequate time on your calendar to ensure that they get done. However, the next thing you know, the day is over and you haven't even gotten halfway through the first item on your list. So frustrating! Am I right?

If you're anything like me, you can easily get derailed by the multitude of distractions and disruptions that can occur on any given day, especially when working from home. Can you hear the laundry, dirty dishes, and other housework and errands calling your name throughout the day? Don't even get me started on social media and the black hole that can become! Even the most diligent among us lose a significant amount of productivity from the constant context-switching that occurs throughout the day....Thanks technology!

So what's a distracted mompreneur to do?

Awareness is the first step to overcoming these time-sucks. Often, we don't even realize we're falling victim to these distractions until after the fact. As mompreneurs, we feel this compelling need to be able to do it all—be the supermom and keep all the plates spinning in the air, all the while, running a successful business. We overcommit and often allow others' needs to surpass our own. Sometimes we utilize these time-sucks as a way of procrastinating from tackling the more difficult or less desirable tasks. What are your blind spots? Being aware of these saboteurs and planning on how to deal with them will help you to be better prepared when they show up.

One activity that I employ with my mompreneur clients that really helps concretely see where the sneaky time-sucks are is to conduct a time audit of a typical week and see where you are spending your time each day.

Next, categorize activities into buckets like personal, family, work (which can be further broken down into meetings, business development, administrative tasks, servicing clients, content creation, etc.). Look for trends. For example, you might find that you waste a lot of time constantly switching from one task to another throughout the day. One minute you might be looking up a contact on LinkedIn and the next thing you know, you're reading an interesting article you found in your newsfeed and forgot all about what you went to LinkedIn for in the first place! Sound familiar?

Find opportunities to group similar activities together by time-blocking. For example, you might reserve early mornings for personal time to work out, meditate, or whatever else you need to do for yourself, and reserve your evenings for focused family time. Perhaps certain days of the week are dedicated to business development activities.

Notice those things you spend time on that you don't enjoy or that could be done equally well or better by someone else. Where are you overcommitting? You should strive to spend the majority of your time on those tasks that you are uniquely qualified to do, play to your strengths, or bring you joy or pleasure. Everything else, consider dumping, delegating, delaying, or outsourcing.

Finally, when you look at your time audit, what did you notice that is MISSING? What are you not getting done that needs to get done, or what are you spending too little time on that you should be spending MORE time on? Ask yourself, "Am I avoiding any difficult tasks by busying myself with other activities?" If it's something that needs to be done now and can't be delegated or outsourced, it may be a matter of building up some momentum to get yourself started. Tell yourself that you'll work on it for only 10 minutes. You will likely find that this small start can be just what you need to get over the hump, keep on going, and knock it out!

You won't be able to eliminate 100% of the distractions that will inevitably occur, but once we acknowledge that eliminating distractions allows us to work smarter and not harder, it can be much easier to stay on track. Taking the time to analyze how you spend your time and identifying ways to optimize through time-blocking, outsourcing, or just plain tricking ourselves into "kissing the frog" can help establish those boundaries and improve your productivity so you have more time to do the things you love!

STEP 3: Let Your Light Shine!

Own your worth and reclaim your power. Seriously, as mompreneurs we often downplay our importance and relinquish our power to fit in or feel accepted. Do you let clients and family members diminish your value?

Let's face it, it is tough playing both the supermom and the savvy business owner role. I get it. We often feel like we don't fully fit in either world or we can't let our whole self show up at home or at work. We want to be nurturing as a mom but tough as a business owner, and we often feel conflicted from the demands and pressures of these seemingly contradictory roles.

Our boundaries are constantly being tested and we can often feel marginalized when a client asks us to discount our price, we feel pressure to volunteer, scope creep occurs on a project, or when our children look to us as the default parent on most things just because we work from home the majority of the time or are our own boss. No, we aren't just sitting at home all day watching talk shows and eating bon-bons!

What's worse, we often justify it to ourselves whenever we allow a breach of our boundaries. We want to be seen as a team player, we believe it will benefit our client or child, we don't want to lose the client, etc. While those things may be true, the harsh reality is there's a tradeoff occurring. You are taking time and attention away from what truly matters to you (remember Step 1: Follow your heart?). If you stray too far from your heart in your day-to-day actions, you can be left feeling resentful and slowly erode your self-confidence and worth.

STOP IT, right now! It is time you see your multifaceted greatness as a true asset that you should leverage. You are worth it! You have far too much to offer the world for you not to be seen, heard, and followed.

You have more power than you realize. There are many sources of power we can draw upon, many of which we often overlook. For example, you can use direct power to stand your ground on your pricing with a client. You don't have to justify your pricing to them. Know and believe in the value you provide, adequately communicate that value to your client, and be prepared to walk away. You'd be amazed at how many of them will come chasing after you once you do! And even if they don't, no makes way for yes—there are plenty of other clients who see your value and would love the opportunity to work with you!

Use relationship power with your family to reset roles and responsibilities. Gain alignment with family members so that everyone understands and respects that you are a working parent. Not every task is worth your time. Divvy up family responsibilities in a way that leverages the strengths of each person and lessens your burden (and teaches your children important life skills and independence too!).

Can you see how, by using these forms of power, you can reclaim your worth, demand respect for your boundaries, gain buy-in for your ideas, and let your light shine? Reflect on the following questions to help you identify areas for development:

- How do you allow clients and family members to diminish your value?
- What stories are you telling yourself to justify your boundaries being breached?

STEP 4: Speak Up! What's That?

I can't hear you! Now that you have reclaimed your power and know your worth, don't hold back; use it to drive conversations to ensure your clients and family understand the value you bring, while reinforcing your boundaries along the way.

Many of my clients struggle with prioritizing their own personal needs. They work long (and late) hours, put their personal relationships on the back burner, blow off scheduled workouts or dinner dates to accommodate meetings that just can't wait, regularly eat a hurried lunch during back-to-back meetings each day...the list goes on. The end result: they resent the little time they have for themselves and their families and are on the fast track to burnout. Any of this sounding familiar?

Let me introduce you to a very powerful word: NO.

So many of us just don't use it enough because we're afraid of being perceived as lazy, uncooperative, or just plain rude. Don't get me wrong, there's definitely a rude way to say no, but there are plenty of ways to say no gracefully, without damaging the relationship in the process. Some strategies to consider:

The power of the "soft no". Essentially, you are saying no, but you offer an alternative. For example, let's say you are asked to chair an event at your kid's school. You could respond with, "My plate is quite full at the moment and I'm not able to devote the time required to chair the event, but I'd be happy to help out at the event itself for a few hours." This soft no allows you to honor your heart and where you really want to spend your time, while preserving the relationship.

The power of the pause. Human beings are naturally uncomfortable with long, awkward periods of silence and always feel the need to fill the void. So, the next time you receive a request (in person or over the phone), don't respond right away. Allow for the pause (count to at least 5) and wait for the other person to fill the void. You'd be amazed at how many people will negotiate themselves down or give you an out when you pause.

Make "no" your default answer. We're also *unaccustomed* to saying no. The more we practice saying it, the easier it gets. Consider making "no" your default answer to any question and then allow yourself to be talked into a yes.

What about times when you need to advocate for yourself and it isn't about just saying "no"? This is where being very clear with your heart's desires and knowing your worth comes into play. It is your responsibility to educate your family and your clients on your boundaries in order to uphold them.

For example, when one of my clients first started her business, she would work wherever made sense around the house or at a client site. Years later, with the majority of her working hours at home, she established a workspace in her home and let her family know that her workspace is a 'no fly' zone. If the door is closed, it means she is working and can't be disturbed. Little things like this can make all the difference in receiving the respect you deserve and helping your family recognize that you are working just as hard as someone who works from an office outside the home, and I would argue that you likely work harder than them!

Identify one thing you can say "no" to today and one thing you can do to establish and communicate your value with your clients and your family.

STEP 5: Keep Your Antenna Up

Obviously, none of us are perfect and we're all going to slip up sometimes. But, in general, maintaining your boundaries needs to be continually practiced and refined over time. Consistency is your friend!

It's easy to let our guard down and let things slide, not only in our business or at home, but in all aspects of our lives. We can often identify our weak spots where we might be more vulnerable than others. Are there particular areas where you find that you allow people to trample all over you? Your kids? Clients? Extended family? Certain friends (you know the one!)? Complete strangers?

How about the volunteer trap for those of you with school-aged kiddos? You find yourself torn; you want to help out and have extreme FOMO, yet you can easily become overcommitted if you're not careful. It is important for you to remain vigilant in maintaining your boundaries so that you don't become overwhelmed or compromise on your priorities (back to checking in with your heart).

How about THAT client? You know the one who regularly uses up more of your time than they pay for or constantly tries to get you to work on areas that are out of the scope of your agreement. Why do we ever put up with this type of client behavior?

We all have our vulnerable areas, it's just a matter of knowing where they are and proactively assessing what we can do to remain vigilant in maintaining healthy boundaries. It's not easy, but it is possible. Once you've identified the usual suspects, think about how it starts. It may not be obvious at first, but there can be early warning signs that can clue us in before it becomes a pattern or habit that's harder to break. For example, do you find you say to yourself, "Just this one time, " or does your gut tell you no, but you are tempted to ignore the warning? Think about the precedent you are setting when allowing this boundary to be breached and how difficult it will be to undo in the future.

Once you see the early warning sign(s), consider the prior 4 steps and ask yourself the following questions:
- How is this decision or action going to make me feel? Does it align with my heart?
- Am I falling victim to one of my time-sucks?
- Am I not seeing my worth and claiming my power?
- Do I need to speak up? Are there certain individuals who I need to level-set with?

What is one step you can take in the next day or so to remain alert to the usual suspects that are likely to encroach and push your boundaries in the near future? What sort of 'early detection' system can you put into place to combat the initial slide?

I hope you can see that by establishing clear and healthy boundaries you will be able to have the thriving business you've always wanted without feeling minimized or underappreciated by your clients or your family. And this is what I specialize in. Helping mompreneurs, just like you, thrive and feel confident in their dual roles as business owners and as moms so they can increase their overall impact both in business and at home. I believe that setting boundaries is a critical first step in upping your game for long-term success.

These five steps are a great start, but there's so much more to it! If you're interested in learning more, go to: www.pragmatic-life.com/yes.html

Chapter 19

List Building Lead Magnets

Ruth Stern, MA

ruth@ruthstern.com

I'm Ruth Stern, Business Coach and Mindset Mentor. My mission is to help mompreneurs attract their ideal clients and feel empowered to do the work they love, while making a lucrative income.

The one thing every mompreneur needs to know when she's struggling to attract her ideal client is that an irresistible lead magnet is the best way to build her list with ideal prospective clients without having to pay for ads. **Here are 5 steps to help you do that.**

STEP 1: Identify The Problem You Solve

An irresistible lead magnet acts as a powerful tool in attracting your dream clients. Lead magnets can be a short ebook, pdf checklist, blueprint, etc. A lead magnet is often referred to as a "gift," and I'll use these 2 words interchangeably. The gift should offer them great value and position you as the expert in your field. Your gift must solve a piece of the problem they want help with so they can breathe a little bit easier and can begin to see the possibilities.

In order to receive their gift, your prospects will have to give you their email. You are now creating a list of potential clients who are already interested in what you do. Once someone signs up, you can now send them more tips, strategies, videos etc. that continue to give value and continue to "dial up your authority and leadership," prepping new subscribers to eventually buy.

Email marketing is still one of the most effective ways to market. Email remains a significantly more effective way to acquire customers than social media—

nearly 40 times that of Facebook and Twitter combined. Social media is great for traffic generation, connecting with your audience, posting your free gifts and attracting potential clients. But, ultimately, you want to sell to your clients in your email list, not on social media.

A lead magnet is an inexpensive way to build your list without having to do expensive ads! So, I want to share with you some important things you must have to create an irresistible lead magnet. To create a great lead magnet that people want to open and consume, you need to get clear on some of your niche market's most pressing problems and challenges.

While you can't solve the whole problem in one gift, ask yourself:

- What is one problem that keeps them up at night?
- What small but important step can I help my audience take that will help them move closer to getting this problem resolved and wanting to work with me in some paid capacity in the future?

When you identify one pressing issue and give them some key tips or strategies to solve the problem, they get a quick win! And it also leaves them wanting more and asking themselves 'what else can I learn I learn from this expert?'

Giving something useful and valuable for free is one of the best ways to get attention in a crowded space. You give your potential clients a taste of your expertise and an opportunity to sample what it's like to experience your product or service.

Here's an example: I have an online program called The Client Attraction Blueprint. It is a comprehensive program from A-Z of how to build a thriving business. My free gift could not possibly address all the areas necessary to build a whole program. So, one of my gifts (that leads to this offer) is called, *The Irresistible Client Lead Magnet Checklist: 10X Your List Building Machine!*

I know that a coach trying to grow their business will want to grow their list, so it is a great lead magnet because I know that this person will be interested in my program that helps coaches build their business. In addition, learning how to create an irresistible lead magnet is one of the modules in the bigger program. So my lead magnet outlines the specific steps necessary in creating a lead magnet. If the coach wants to know more, they will be interested in investing in my bigger program.

So, this gift gives insight into solving one part of the problem for the entrepreneur to build her business which is how to build a list and become more visible.

Now it's your turn. Write down 3 of the most pressing problems, struggles, or challenges your niche market faces. Choose one problem you can address that you know is top of mind for them.

STEP 2: Offer The Solution

Once you've identified the problem you know they have, you want to offer solutions for something they can do right now.

For example: you are a nutrition coach and offer a program on eating healthy to gain more energy and vitality. The problem you identify for your lead magnet is: identifying foods that zap your energy. The solution could be: 3 foods you can add to your normal diet to immediately amp up energy.

Now it's your turn. What are 2 or 3 tips/strategies you can offer to help them solve their challenge? Also think of what unique approach or fresh perspective you can bring to the table.

It's very important that you offer what I call your "golden nuggets," meaning your best advice and tips. People can google a lot of information, so you want to really dive deep and ask yourself, what can I share that is unique and extremely helpful to my audience? Your solution may be action steps or mindset shifts or a visualization or an mp3. Get creative with it! And then ask yourself: Would this solution I just offered be something I would do or something that would motivate me? This question helps you move from generic to specific in the advice you offer and helps you design those golden nuggets! And remember, when they consume information and experience they value, you will leave them craving more. And when the time comes for your prospect to be ready to get coached, YOU will be top of mind!

STEP 3: Design A Hot Title

You know how you decide to read a book based on its title? The same is true of your free lead magnet. If your title isn't compelling, people will not sign up for it, even if it's free.

Audiences today are inundated with information from social media and the web. So, you need to capture their attention with a hot title. How do you create a hot sizzling title? A great title either addresses the pain or the solution.

Here are some title examples:
- *3 Big Myths About Healing Depression*—this title addresses the problem
- *How To Create An Irresistible Lead Magnet*—this title addresses the solution

Both are equally effective. Some suggestions to create a hot title include: "How To" titles or titles that include a number (The 3 Best Ways to…. Or 7 Mistakes….)

Notice the difference between these 2 titles and see which one you are drawn to:
- *Create FB Posts To Reach Your Audience*
- *3 Types of FB Posts That Will Engage And Instantly Attract Your Audience*

Which one were you drawn to? Most likely the second one because we used a number. Numbers work well because they tell you that you won't have to do a zillion things. The verbs "engage" and "attract" are stronger words that excite you to want to learn more. The word "instantly" is a winner because it lets you know you can have your challenge solved immediately!

Creating a great title is about using your creative imagination. Just play with it! A great way to create your title is to write as fast as you can. Write at least 10 different ones. Don't judge. Just write. Then you can combine and tweak. When I need help, I survey my social media groups by posting titles and asking for favorites.

Now, it's your turn. Write as fast as you can. Use the "How To" or Numbers suggestion. Write down problem and solution titles—and just play with it!

STEP 4: Decide On The Type of Lead Magnet You Will Create

So, you've created your lead magnet content and now it's time to decide what format you will use to deliver it. There are many types of lead magnets. Some common ones include pdf report, small eBook, video, template, checklist, audio or video series, and many more.

What you decide will be dependent on knowing your audience. Is your audience more of a reader? Do they prefer video or audio? Are they checklist type of people? Whatever type of lead magnet you design, it's important to write in your ideal client's language and address them as if you are speaking to one person.

Write your content without sounding formal or using obvious marketing language. Just be genuine. This is not about you being a great poetic writer. It's about writing from your heart and giving them your best. People love when you're clear so keep it simple!

And the great news is that you can create lead magnets for FREE! For example, there are tons of free apps available for you to create an audio mp3. You can also use your smartphone to create a video which you can download to YouTube for free.

If you don't know how to create a cover image, there are many inexpensive design websites where you can find someone to create a 3D image of your gift. How great is that?

Now it's your turn. As you think about your lead magnet, how do you want to deliver your information? What would be the easiest way for you to deliver and what would your audience most likely consume?

STEP 5: Capture Your Ideal Clients

To bring people to your email list, you need to go to different platforms to connect with others and add your link to your lead magnet.

Core places to post your lead magnet would include: FB pages and groups, FB lives, your website, LinkedIn, Twitter, Instagram, YouTube, Podcasts and Blogs. Any time you speak on an interview or livestream, you can offer your gift. Basically, post your gift wherever your audience hangs out. There are tons of ways to connect and offer your gift!

I have added thousands of new prospects to my email list with YouTube. I create short educational videos and post my link under the video to download free gifts. YouTube became my free online advertiser and continues to be for my business today.

So how do you capture their name and email?
1. First you must have an email server like Mail chimp, A-Weber, etc. so you can collect and send emails.
2. You need to have a lead magnet landing page that includes an opt-in box that will capture their name and email that will connect to your email server. Some of the more popular ones are Leadpages and ClickFunnels. These are reasonably priced software programs that have templates where you easily plug in your information.
3. When you post your gift on the platform, the person clicks the link to get the gift. The landing page pops up and offers them the gift which they receive after they enter their name and email.
4. The next page is a thank you page that immediately pops up and often includes the link to the gift
5. Best practices include also sending an automatic email with the gift link inside as well.

All this is created with your lead pages software which "talks" with your mail server to create this flow. In other words, your mail server and lead magnet landing page integrate together to create this system that works so well. It's your CAPTURE MACHINE! It's very simple to set up as software is so easy to use these days!

Now it's your turn. Write down which platforms you will start advertising your Free Gift on.

Notice that everything I just showed you is organic. It's all free to create your irresistible gift (except for the Leadpage Software). Your investment is small in comparison to what you will receive in return. A lead magnet is really the gift that keeps on giving! It is one of the greatest tools I have used in my business to get seen and grow my list and profits!

Are you ready to build your list with One Irresistible Free Lead Magnet? One that will target your ideal client and will get you paying clients without having to waste money on ads? You have a zillion ways to get it out there. A well planned lead magnet will position you as the leader and expert in your field and offer high value to your audience! Your irresistible lead magnet is truly your list building machine.

I've created a free gift for you that will dive deeper into how to create a hot lead magnet and how to nurture your next step in growing your client base! Your clients are waiting for you, make it easier for them to find you by downloading my free Build Your Irresistible Lead Magnet here:
https://pages.ruthstern.com/client-magnet-free-gift/

Chapter 20

Aligning Your Work and Life

Lisa Duerre

lisa@rldgroupllc.com

My name is Lisa Duerre and I'm an Executive Success Coach and CEO. I inspire moms with careers just like you to stop feeling maxed out and finally live a life you love while doing work that matters. Aligning your work and life is the key to feeling awesome about your career impact and being present for the moments that matter with your loved ones.

The one thing every mompreneur needs to know when she's feeling depleted and overwhelmed (with all there is to running a business and being a parent), is that when you align your work and life, your energy and clarity increases, you're more effective, and you can enjoy your life. **Here are 5 steps to help you do that.**

STEP 1: Know Your Gratitude Story

Here's a question for you. Why did you become an entrepreneur in the first place? For me, entrepreneurship was my kick out of the nest when my daughter was in kindergarten. I wanted to be a Mom and a CEO. It was scary to make that leap! I was a Silicon Valley executive at a great company and the perks were nice. Yet I had no control over my time, and I felt a deep yearning in my soul to do work on my terms. That yearning became a roar when my daughter was five and I found that my mom had only months to live. My soul craved two things: time to be present for the moments that matter with my loved ones and to make a bigger impact in the world by coaching business leaders committed to their careers and families on how to align their work and life.

So, I made the decision to leave my corporate gig and launch my work-from-home CEO+Mom adventure. No, it hasn't been perfect, but wow, I wouldn't change anything. I remember our family driving to Disneyland. We made a planned pitstop so I could grab a coaching call with one of my clients. My husband and our daughter grabbed lunch while I connected with my client from my 'remote office'—our minivan. My client is an Executive Vice President in a major tech company, and I was ready for that call. We didn't skip a beat in our conversation because I had great WiFi, prepared notes and questions, and the space to be present.

That call created a major breakthrough for my client that she still talks about today. I could have let my travel plans delay that time with my client or chose not to go on the trip, but our family was flexible to meet my client's needs and still keep our plans on schedule. I don't think that call—or that breakthrough—would have happened without our flexibility and my clarity on the moments that mattered to me. That win-win is priceless to me.

So why did I tell you this story? Because this is my gratitude story. It's my reminder that being a mompreneur can create those types of amazing memories. As business owners, we have so much flexibility to be present with our kids, our partners and our loved ones in the moments that matter. We get to make an impact on our clients, their customers and the larger community. Here's the deal. When you start with gratitude, you need to be hyper-specific about what you're thankful for and why it matters. What's working well in your business and your life? Every part of life may seem like chaos right now—I get it, but you probably have a lot to be thankful for, right? For example, you have air to breathe, food to eat, a place to sleep, and clothes to wear (and heck, some of us get to wear super comfy clothes 'cause we're working from home).

So, what's YOUR story, Mama? What's a moment in time when you felt really grateful for being a mompreneur and all that entrepreneurship allows for? Take some time to write this down in detail—and know that even the smallest things count! This can really help clarify what's really important to you.

STEP 2: Identify And Eliminate What's Not Working

We know life as a mom with a career is much different than life before kids. Your entire schedule changes along with your body, your sleep, your patience and even your 'need' for a shower. This also means life as a mompreneur may need to look different than if you were an entrepreneur before becoming a mom.

While we intuitively know things need to change when overwhelm hits, it's another thing entirely to proactively make the change! I see this all the time with my clients. As an entrepreneur and Mom, it's really common to think, "I can do it all—I'm Wonder Woman!" Let's be real here, dude, we both know working like you used to before kids isn't realistic. Running your business requires you to be at your best. Putting in a 12-hour workday while trying to be a great mom, a great partner and a halfway-decent friend is not a good idea. That's a guaranteed way for your life to quickly spiral out of control.

So, we try to make compromises. "I'll just get up earlier before the kids wake up." "I'll just exercise on the weekend." "It's okay if I skip lunch; it's not a big deal." Newsflash: it is a big deal when we ignore self-care and put our needs on the back burner. It's a recipe for burnout—believe me, I know. I work with women all the time that feel lost as a mom, a wife, a business leader and a human being when they put their needs aside while trying to be Wonder Woman.

I guide my clients to find what works for them. It's important to keep a pulse on what lights you up as a mom, as a woman and as an entrepreneur. Pssst… here's the deal…you own your business. You have the chance to organize your life how you want, so enjoy that freedom.

If we're going to truly align our work with our life goals, we need to identify and eliminate what's not working for us as business owners. Make a list of what's not working. Write out exactly how each of these things makes you feel. Be painfully honest—nobody else needs to see your list. For example:

- I'm doing a terrible job with closing on sales calls with prospects.
- My flower bed in the front yard is constantly filled with weeds.
- My child is not sleeping well—heck our whole family isn't sleeping well.

Now, go through every task on your list, even if it's a hundred things, and make a decision about it. Take steps to eliminate it, delegate it, or put it "on hold." We'll deal with the tasks that are "on hold" in the next step.

STEP 3: Acknowledge What You're Tolerating *Without* Shaming Yourself

Dude, guess what mompreneurs don't need more of in life? Shame and judgment. And yet, we tolerate so much shame—"I'm not good enough…."; "Others have it worse than me…."; "I should be more grateful—so many others don't have what I have…."; or, "Who do you think you are? Are you really that special trying to run your own business?" If any of those sound familiar, that's the voice of shame and judgment.

As moms, we can experience shame from every direction—other moms, our partners, our kids, our family members, our neighbors, even complete strangers at the grocery store when our kid takes a tantrum to that level. This can also be true as entrepreneurs. If your business isn't exactly where you want it to be, sometimes those closest to us will advise us to "give up and get a REAL job."

The worst part is we're often the ones shaming ourselves the most. Even though you may love building your business and connecting with other amazing people online, you may fall prey to the 'should-isms': you should post more, you should respond to emails faster, you should go to more events, you should speak on more stages.

This leads us away from what we want and keeps us firmly stuck in what we think we should do…mistakenly thinking that we aren't doing enough. This leads to a vicious cycle of shame and self judgment which can trample our boundaries and impact our relationships at home. It's so easy to get caught up in the liking, tweeting, posting, sharing, sheer exhaustion of marketing your business from the comfort of your phone. Have you ever had your child ask you, "Why are you on your phone again?" Were you cringing inside as you firmly explained you were working while posting social media? If that feels familiar, you are intimately familiar with shame.

So, how do you silence the shame and create a plan for aligning your work with your life? Here's an exercise I do with my clients. Let's go back to your list from Step 2. You already identified tasks on that list that you are taking action to eliminate or delegate. This will make you feel much more in control of your time and your happiness. So, let's focus on the tasks that are left "on hold." These are tasks that you are either not willing or not capable of giving up right now but still need to get done. Many tasks on the list will resolve themselves in time. Others you will be able to eliminate or delegate in the future—your list is evolving and it's important to maintain your perspective! Try to get to a place where you are accepting of where you are right now in the development of your business and the stage of motherhood that you are in.

STEP 4: Know What Lights You Up

You now have a list of what you don't exactly love doing, but that you are willing to accept as part of this amazing life that you are grateful for. Now let me ask you...do you also know what lights you up? What gets you excited? What do you love doing so much that you lose track of time? Knowing what lights you up is the clarity you need to start aligning your work and life.

When did you last get some good Mama Time? As business owners and moms, we're accustomed to spending every part of our energy and focus without taking time to simply "be." Here's a tip: Get out into the sunshine, breathe deep, and enjoy some fresh air. Count the stars, savor your favorite drink on the porch, take a hot bath, and give yourself the time and space to rest. Whatever gets you out of your head and into your heart is what I'm talking about here. Taking time for yourself can give you the mental clarity you need to know what you truly want out of life and for your business. When you quiet yourself and connect with your heart, you can hear the whispers of your soul. This is the birthplace of innovation and clarity.

I like to have my clients regularly do visualization exercises. These can be quick and powerful motivators that keep us on track and in alignment. While in a quiet space, close your eyes and begin to imagine success on your terms. What would having your work and your life in alignment mean for you? For each of us, our dream is different. This is very personal. As you envision your dream life, pay special attention to what feelings it evokes. So many believe it is things that we want, but what we really want is the experience of feeling a certain way. Your dreams are fueled by your desires and feelings. This is what I want you to tap into when you visualize.

The real power is in being clear on how aligning your work with your life will make you feel. If your work isn't aligned with the life you desire, those negative feelings will manifest in this step. Pay attention when they do—and make decisions more in line with your soul's desires. Be aware of this reality—you'll need to repeat steps 1-4 when this happens (and it will happen), so doing this process in a journal can be very helpful so you can reflect on what you've already accomplished. Do not skip Step 5 though, as it is critical to your success in aligning your work and life.

STEP 5: Support Is Everything

It's amazing to me how many business owners start their businesses by adopting the habits and behaviors of the corporate world. Maybe you still use Outlook or Office 365. Maybe you use the same invoicing system as your corporate job used. Maybe your business cards look like your old ones. And yet, many entrepreneurs don't see the need for the same type of support the corporate world provides. They just jump into entrepreneurship without acknowledging that it is a completely different experience. As employees, we have the support of structure and mentors. Your roles and responsibilities are clearly defined. There are systems in place and the path has been clearly laid out for you. Tell me Mama, who supports you in your business?

Support can be the difference-maker for so many mompreneurs. I've seen a much higher success rate with mompreneurs skyrocketing their success and creating amazing lives and businesses once they invest in the proper support. The mompreneurs who try to do it on their own can be successful, but the road is longer and harder without support.

A coach can help you get clear on what's working and what's not. They guide you in identifying a better way to do work you love so you can be present for the moments that matter. An awesome coach will support you with business aspects and your mindset. As a mompreneur, I suggest you find a coach that helps parents committed to their careers and families, as your situation is a bit more complex (as you already know). When looking for a great coach, you need to know they've been where you are and know how to navigate the terrain so that they can help get you where you want to go with their support. There are a lot of coaches who hide behind great marketing materials and loads of hype, but can they produce results? Find someone with the track record to match their message and be sure you feel comfortable with their personality. In addition, I suggest you find someone to guide you and your business who can ask tough questions and hold you accountable to your dreams while providing insight, tools, and resources to align your work and life. Here's a really important tip for you when working with a coach: be completely vulnerable about where you're at with your life and business. Share all of your fears, questions, concerns, and details with them. When you do that though, be aware of this pitfall...you're probably going to feel some shame. Fight that shame! Give yourself some grace, because no one who truly matters expects you to have it all together.

If you're not ready to hire a coach yet, that's okay, start with a mentor as they are free. Ask them to hold you accountable and ask them to make recommendations. The same tips I gave you above regarding working with a coach apply here, too. Be completely vulnerable about where you're at with your life and business. Otherwise, you are wasting their time and yours. A mentor or a coach can only really support you if you're real with them.

You can align your work and your life AND it's so worth it. If after working through these 5 steps, you are wanting more, go to: www.lisaduerre.com/ready

Chapter 21

Gracefully Support Your Aging Parents

Lori LeCarl

5steps2renewYOU@gmail.com

My name is Lori LeCarl. I'm a Life Coach supporting devoted daughters. I help "stretched too thin" mompreneurs replenish, rebalance and renew so you can stop the overwhelm of the never ending responsibilities of your children, your parents, and your clients. My mission is to guide you in creating space for you to serve your loved ones and have more quality time with them, while also having quality time to renew yourself, pursue your passion, and live your best life.

The one thing every mompreneur needs to know when she's frazzled and exhausted because she's feeling pulled in so many directions is that she needs to "love up" herself as much as she's "loving-up" everyone else. **Here are 5 steps to help you do that.**

STEP 1: Re-align with The Divine YOUniverse

Bouncing back and forth as you support your children, your clients, and your parents is taking a serious toll on you on every level, and simply put, you are doing so at your own peril. Chances are that your spirit is depleted, so nourishing your spirit is the best place to start reversing the tide in your favor. As you re-align with, and open up to, your Divine self (be it God, Love, Peace, a Higher Power…however you define it and experience it) you'll tap into a powerful energy that will transform whatever you believe it can transform. Several wonderful things happen when you nourish your spirit. You feel better. You set other positive changes into motion, within and around you. Plus, because of the ripple effect, those around you reap the benefits when you nourish your spirit…that means your children, your clients, and your parents. And, guess what? Just like when one boat rises, they all do—when your vibration rises, so does theirs! The good that you create by nourishing your spirit spreads out to everyone in your family and also comes back to you. You will create a beautiful circle of ever-increasing love, peace, harmony, joy, fun, etc. weaving in and out of each individual family member, your family as a whole, AND rippling out into The Universe. "But, wait a minute!" you say, "I can't add another thing to my already overflowing plate!" Well, I have great news for you, you don't have to. You can nourish your spirit and raise your vibration while doing other things. That's right, you don't need to add it to your mile- long to-do list! Let's face it, you have multi-tasking down pat. All you need to do, if you so choose, is to allow a few simple mantras to play in the back of your mind.

- I love you…
- I am sorry…
- Please forgive me…
- Thank you.

You may recognize these statements as the basic phrases of an ancient Hawaiian process called Ho'oponopono. But you don't need to be familiar with this process, you just need to know that it works. For over a decade, I've been using this process daily. I use "I love you" and "thank you" more than I use the other two phrases. Though all four phrases are extremely profound *and* powerful I find going through my day with "I love you" and "thank you" replaying in my head prepares a path of greater good for me that shows up in a myriad of ways and even opens doors for wonderful surprises. I have my clients use the phrases in any order and pick the ones that really resonate with them. When they have a negative thought or feeling toward someone, respond in an unkind way, have concerns about someone they love, or start worrying about money, I have them repeat the mantra, "*I am sorry, please forgive me*" in their head. When appropriate, I have them add, "*thank you.*" If appropriate, I also have them add, "*I love you.*" Sometimes, I suggest they say "I'm sorry" directly. The truth is, you are probably already using these phrases at various times throughout your day and receiving benefits from doing so. Now imagine the BIG benefits that you will experience if you are thinking *I love you* or thank you as a mantra to help you navigate throughout your day. You can have a specific person (including yourself) and/or any situation in mind while you're using these mantras, but it's not necessary. These mantras are transformative either way as they increase your inner peace. When you're experiencing inner peace, no matter what's happening around you, there are no limits to what you can achieve and receive. There's no such thing as doing it wrong.

I promised you could multitask while nourishing your spirit, and I wasn't kidding! These mantras can play in the back of your mind while driving, shopping, showering, brushing your teeth, exercising, watching TV, reading your emails—just about anything! Pick just one activity when you can use the mantra and then add other activities at a pace that's comfortable for you. Work your way up to doing it daily. The key is consistency. Patience really helps, as well, since the breakthroughs don't necessarily happen according to our timeframe.

STEP 2: Do Your Best & Let Experts Do the Rest

You're doing your best and giving your best to your children, parents, and clients at a mighty high cost to your well-being. The bottom line is you can't do it all. When you're spread too thin, you aren't firing on all cylinders. You're in a cycle of too little sleep, too much rushing, too little time in the day, too much to do, too little time off, and it's all too much. So here's the million dollar question. What tasks, chores, or other responsibilities can you hire other people to do? Whether it's for you, your children, your parents, your house, or your business, there are experts who would gladly take some responsibilities off your plate. I suggest you start with your biggest energy drainer. Whatever that is for you, there is a right and perfect person who can handle it for you. Next, take a look at your biggest time waster. Your biggest energy and time waster may be one and the same. For me, house cleaning is too draining on both counts, so I have someone that comes regularly. I also have a landscaper for lawn care and snow removal. Getting help, or more help with household chores frees up some of your valuable time and energy. Whether it's house cleaning, laundry, cooking, making school lunches, running errands, picking up after your kids, grocery shopping or lawn care. Taking whatever you can off of your overloaded plate is a BIG deal. There are awesome professionals who can help your children with homework, drive them to and from school, sports, other activities, and more. Some of these things you may want to do yourself; however, if you are rushed or stressed out doing any of these, it may be better for you and your child to have someone else do it. You'll save time and energy while also reducing your stress level, and theirs. Your opportunities to connect in more enjoyable, carefree ways grow organically. In the same way, there are also lots of caregivers who can lighten your load as a devoted daughter. From companionship to driving your parents to appointments, taking them shopping, or maybe even doing the shopping for them. From adult day care centers to in-home care providers to visiting nurses. There's "round the clock" care at home or in assisted living facilities. There's respite care, for when you need some time off or are going on vacation. As a daughter, I can tell you that these options are golden. My mom enjoyed an adult day care program for a while. They picked her up and brought her home each day. As the dementia worsened, my mom became more of a "flight risk" and they got tired of running down the street to find her, so we had caregivers come to the house. We gradually added days and hours to the caregivers' schedules and eventually had coverage 22 hours/day. In March of 2018, I moved her into the memory care unit of an assisted living facility, and she is so happy, comfortable and well taken care of. It was such a tough decision to make, and I probably should have done it sooner, but in the end, it proved to be the best course of action. Though I oversee and make decisions regarding her care and support her in other ways, I get to spend my visit loving her and being fully present in the moment. I'm out from under the strain and burden of caregiving responsibilities. Believe me, whatever it is you are going through, I've either gone through it myself or have coached my clients through it. At my suggestion, my clients hire assistants to go through their parent's mail weekly, handle their paperwork, make calls when needed, deposits checks, and more. These are major time and energy drainers that you will be so grateful to be free of. My point is there is help "out there." There are people who are well suited for what you need. Ask around—friends, neighbors, doctors, lawyers, clergy, others that you trust. The same is true for your business. Get referrals for virtual assistants, marketing strategists, copywriters, personal assistants, social media experts, and the like. Outsourcing whatever you can afford and feel comfortable with, provides more time and energy for the tasks that directly increase your sales and service your clients at a higher level.

Do yourself a favor and make a list of what you do on a regular basis at home, for your children, for your parents, in your business, etc. Then take a good look at your list and see what you can hand off to someone else. Understand that your well-being is dependent upon reducing your responsibilities and increasing the time and energy you devote to yourself.

STEP 3: Give Yourself a "Time Out"

That's right! Now that you have some great experts in place to shrink your workload and raise your vibration some more, you get to have a few minutes to yourself. WOO HOO! Your "time out" a.k.a. pressing the PAUSE button on your responsibilities will refuel your mind, body, and spirit. There is an unfoldment that takes place as you unwind and it goes something like this: you catch your breath and release stress, your spirit starts to soar and your sense of freedom expands, overwhelm loosens its grip and peace of mind makes a comeback, the heavy weight of responsibility begins to melt away and greater clarity steps forward. Of course, everyone's experience is different, but rest assured, taking several 5-10 minute "time outs" throughout your day will do you a world of good. Here are some ideas on what to do during your time-outs: breathe deeply and consciously, get out in nature, sing, hum, dance, whistle, hydrate, meditate, take a short walk, connect with a supportive family member or friend, have a healthy snack, drink a cup of tea, enjoy the silence, read something inspirational, write a poem, enjoy a few moments of doing nothing, or do whatever else your heart desires. Spend that time doing whatever floats your boat and energizes you. I suggest my clients plan their time outs and schedule them into their day by adding it to their calendar or setting an alarm on their phone to remind them to take this time for themselves. Take this time for yourself now and add some "time outs" to your schedule, and if you can work your way up to at least 2-3 of them each day, the benefits will be more consistent and obvious.

STEP 4: Dare To Take Care Of YOU First

This is the really juicy step! Since you've delegated some of your responsibilities AND are now in the habit of scheduling regular "time outs" to PAUSE, breathe and just be in the present moment, the next step is plugging in some much deserved "me time." This is where you get to have some real quality time with yourself and with others too. The goal is to enhance and increase your experiences of love, joy, peace, fun, relaxation, laughter, and so on. Swimming, especially outdoors, is incredibly soul satisfying for me and I strive to swim every day during pool season. I release so much stress and negativity when I swim. I thoroughly enjoy it and it energizes me on every level. And as my thinking gets clearer again, a plethora of good ideas and solutions come to mind. I'm like a new person when I get out of the pool. I occasionally take my grandchildren overnight to a local hotel during the off-season and it's all about swimming. We have a ball and feel great for days after. Last winter I realized that we need to do that more often. And we are…yippee!

What feeds YOUR soul…brings you joy…makes you laugh…lights you up… makes your heart sing? Here are some different activities my clients enjoy: massage, Reiki, acupuncture, E.F.T. (a.k.a. tapping), going out with friends, a dance or painting class, a meditation group, soaking up the sun with a good book (or a nap, LOL), a walk on the beach or in the woods, fun times with your kids, a day out, a weekend away, and how about a vacation?!? Don't delay, put something on your calendar today. And keep the momentum going. You need it, you deserve it, and remember the ripple effect—everyone around you benefits, and then it comes back to you.

STEP 5: Use A Natural Remedy To Rescue You

There are a number of natural remedies, as you may well know, but I'd like to focus on my favorite one. It's my #1 "go to" product because it has withstood the test of time, no matter what's been going on in my life since the early 1990s. I recommend *Rescue Remedy* to every one of my clients and they all rave about it. It's a combination of 5 Bach Flower Essences that will work for you, your children, your parents, your pets and even your plants. It's not a vitamin or a supplement, just simply the essence (vibration) of beneficial plants. *Rescue Remedy* does contain a small amount of alcohol for preservation, but there is a *Rescue Remedy* formula available for *kids*, and for pets, without the alcohol. You can find it at most health food or vitamin stores or online. Besides the liquid (drops), it comes in many other forms these days such as spray, gum, a cream, pastilles, a sleep formula, and more. My grandkids love the pastilles, I prefer the liquid, but my clients each have their own favorite form. With the liquid, only 4 drops are needed and can be put directly on your tongue, put in a beverage and even added to a bathtub full of water. You can also put it directly on your skin. *Rescue Remedy* does exactly what the name indicates, it rescues you from any emotional distress, upset, exhaustion on any level, and the like. The sooner you start to use it when something comes up, the better. Since physical difficulties can cause emotional distress, it's also great to use during illness, after any type of accident and when experiencing jet lag. During times of intense negative emotions, it can be taken as frequently as every 15 minutes and it's easy to carry in a purse. When needed, I put 4 drops in a small amount of water and drink it all, or I'll put 4 drops in a full glass of water or water bottle and sip on it throughout the day. Do yourself a favor and check it out. My clients and I use *Rescue Remedy* regularly and we love the subtle shift it offers us to continue along our day in a calm and focused way.

These steps work when you work them. I share them with you because they work for me and countless others in my circle. I wholeheartedly believe that re-aligning with your Divine self is the most crucial step in making the positive changes you desire for yourself, your situation, your family, your business, and more. Ho'oponopono is the simplest and easiest way to do that. Focusing on and expressing love and gratitude throughout your day is powerful beyond words and greatly amplifies your efforts to find the right people to take on the responsibilities you're looking to delegate. Love and gratitude will pave the way to meaningful and fulfilling "time outs" and empower you to take care of YOU first AND connect you to the most relaxing, fun, joy filled, peaceful and soul enriching activities for YOU. Love and gratitude can even guide you to the support that's perfect for you, be it people or the use of Rescue Remedy and/or any other natural remedy that resonates with you. Ho'oponopono will support you in ways you can't yet imagine as you support your loved ones! If you are truly looking for positive changes within and around you, then you owe it to yourself to try these 5 steps on for size and really give them a chance to show you what they can do for you.

If you are in need of further support, I'd be honored to speak with you. Schedule a complimentary strategy session with me: https://LoriLeCarl.as.me/

Chapter 22

Discover Endless Content Topics

Esther Shelley

esther@maxyourimpact.com

My name is Esther Shelley. As a Business Content Coach, I help overwhelmed mompreneurs find and use the right content that will attract their ideal client so that you can stop wasting time and start making money. My mission is to help you grow your business by helping you tap into a never-ending stream of content, so you never have to worry about staring at a blank screen again.

The one thing every mompreneur needs to know when she's overwhelmed and struggling to develop relevant content for her business is that it's easy once you have a strategy in place. **Here are 5 steps to help you do that.**

STEP 1: Extract Content From The Experts

As mompreneurs, you probably don't have the time to ethically extract the secrets of others. It takes time to comb through articles and podcasts and put your own spin on them. Maybe you don't have the money to spend on high-end research experts to help you identify what your clients are desperately searching for. But many successful influencers in your field do have the money to pay those high-end experts and you can leverage this information by beginning to follow them. Sign up for their free Facebook group and join their mailing lists by signing up for their freebies or lead magnets. Once you begin getting their emails, notice the topics they focus on. Their teams have already tested the waters, have heard what your mutual market is craving, and are rushing to fill that need. Once you know the topic, you can add your spin on it with a healthy dose of your secret sauce to make it your own. When you find a topic that you like, copy and paste the topic into a word doc or excel file which will become your Content Bank. This will be where you collect all of your content ideas. In your Content Bank, include key points, and any cool phrases you like. Each content topic will become the basis of a piece of content for you in the future. When you are ready to use that topic, dress it up with language that is uniquely yours and that resonates with your tribe. Fill it with how your solution solves your client's pain points. You can use this content in a multitude of ways. Add your unique flavor with stories and experiences that help your readers relate to the outcome. You can use this content in a blog post, on a livestream, in an upload to your YouTube channel, on a podcast, or in an email to your own list! Can you see how easy it is to find hot topics in this way? Make it a practice to add to your Content Bank each day. Here are some action steps you can take to make this easier for you:

- Dedicate an email address for this purpose so that they are easy to find.
- Follow 5 high-end influencers today by downloading all their freebies and joining their free Facebook groups.
- Follow a few up-and-coming influencers to build relationships for future networking.

STEP 2: Hear The Heart-Language Of Your Tribe

Once you've already put in the effort of finding influencers and joining their free Facebook Groups, it is time to start connecting with the members in the groups. While following the group guidelines, start asking questions with a particular goal in mind—to learn who they really are and what they really need. What you want to know is how your clients describe their struggles—even if you think you know what their struggle is. The important part of this exercise is that you catch the words they use to describe their struggle. Be on the lookout for feeling words and words that are used repeatedly. What you are listening for are snippets and phrases that your ideal clients typically use when they speak informally within groups of their peers. In step 1, you researched to figure out the hottest topics that will interest your clients. Now, it's time to flesh these out in a way that tugs at their heartstrings so that they get emotionally connected to you. Without offering them support, here are some questions you can ask:

- If you needed help with your area of expertise, where would you find it?
- Has anyone here dealt with the problem you solve; how did you solve it?
- Does the problem your clients face ever frustrate you?

This strategy is like 'mining for gold'. Try to develop the conversations by prodding them to go deeper. When they reply to you, you can ask them questions that go deeper. Questions like:

- And then what happened?
- What did that mean for you?
- What else happened as a result of that?

Again, use the snippet and phrases found in the comments to add to your topic choices. Keep a list of 10 questions and track which groups you are asking which question. You don't want to ask the same question in the same group time and time again! When you land on a great topic that gets a lot of engagement, then you know you have a winner! Add that topic to your content bank spreadsheet for future content development.

STEP 3: Look For Content Topic Ideas Everywhere

Once you know that you can find content topic ideas anywhere, you will begin to see content topic ideas everywhere. There are so many free sources available for us to find low-hanging fruit. For example, you can do a search on your topic in podcasts. When you find a successful podcaster that you resonate with, look at their interview topics. Bam! There are your topic ideas to add to your Content Bank! You can go to YouTube and put in your keywords and see what the most popular YouTube videos are. Whatever people are watching is what they are interested in. What about search engines? Google is amazing...but if you use different search engines, that will multiply your answers. Type in the words, "How can I (and your solution)" and you will see a number of topic ideas offered to you! Summits are an amazing resource. Many summits will have 40 or more experts speaking on one topic. Find summits that focus on YOUR topic and then look at what the experts are talking about. Each expert will speak on a different subtopic of interest. That means that ONE summit can yield 40 different content topics for you! Do you see where I am going with this? These are all available opportunities for you that are really right in front of your nose. When you start looking at it this way, you will start to see these topics everywhere! Start with these ideas I gave you, but also commit to keeping your eyes open for other content ideas! And keep your Content Bank growing!

STEP 4: Use Interviews

You will need to interview your prospective ideal client to gather valuable information. Find people that are similar to the type of person who would be buying your program or service and ask them if you can interview them for about 15 minutes. Ask them to answer you without hesitation and to tell you whatever comes to mind. These are open ended questions and you want to get them to speak freely so they get really comfortable and speak naturally. Tell your interviewee the problem you solve to define the context of your line of questioning. Then you can begin your questions.

- How is this problem impacting your life, your business, your family, your social life, your self-esteem?
- How else is this problem affecting your relationships and your life?

You want to really poke them so that they are feeling emotional about this. Then flip the switch and ask them questions about what their best outcome would look like.

- How would your life change if this problem were solved?
- How would that change your life, your business, your family, your social life, your retirement goals, your self-esteem?
- What else would change for you?

What you are listening for is repetition. Identify the 6 or 7 phrases or snippets that make up their dreams and challenges and all the ways your solution impacts them. This will help you identify the other problems you are solving for them. When we solve one problem, our solution impacts many other areas of their life. This is what you want to focus on in your interview. Each additional problem that you solve is another topic to add to your content bank! For example, I am a Content Creation Coach and I help mompreneurs create content. When a coach hires me, they can expect that they will learn how to develop tons of content ideas to fill their visibility calendar. However, I know that when I am able to simplify their business, and I take that headache off their plate, they are now happier in their business. So, an additional outcome could be that they have more energy to devote to their clients and their family. Knowing this, I can add content to my calendar highlighting how great it is to have extra energy to spend on yourself and your family. I also know that now that they no longer have to spend so much time on finding content, they can more easily focus on serving their clients and signing up new clients. This means that an additional outcome would be that they can look forward to making more money. With this information, I can create content around how much easier it is to grow your business when you have the time to devote to servicing your clients and new client acquisition.

Can you see how you can find different topics that relate to your offer as you are gathering information from your interviewee?

STEP 5: Survey Your List

The interview process was a very valuable step in amassing content topics. Because your interviewees were asked open ended questions, the answers could really be anything. What you were looking for was the repetition. Now that you know the 6 or 7 phrases or snippets that make up their dreams and challenges and all the ways your solution impacts them, it's time to create a very strategic survey. The purpose of the survey is to have them choose an answer from a finite amount of options. This will make it easier for you to see which topics are the most popular. Of course, you can create content around all of the topics, but this will help you easily rank them from hottest to coldest. The trick here is to offer less than 6 options and to only ask ONE question each time. If they see a bunch of questions with too many options, you are likely to get fewer responses. You want it to be as easy as possible for them to help you do your research. Ask ONE question and give them 6 very specific answer options. Ask them to choose only ONE answer. Tell them you understand that there may be many answers that they relate to, but you want them to choose the one that resonates the most. When you are creating a survey, make sure you choose the setting that restricts multiple answers. There are many apps that will allow you to create forms, choose one that has that setting available. Use the answers you gathered from the interview as the answer option for your survey. These surveys will give you a tremendous amount of insight for more topics. Here are three questions for you to start with and then develop your own as you see fit:

1. When it comes to your area of expertise, which of the following best describes what got you stuck?
2. What do you find most frustrating about their challenge?
3. Besides the obvious outcome of what the promise of your solution is, how else would that impact your life?

Consistently using these 5 strategies will ensure that you never run out of material and you always have a constant stream of content topics geared to your best client!

If you are ready for more ways to simplify your business with a never ending stream of hot topics, visit my website: www.maxyourimpact.com/esthershelley

Chapter 23
Money-Making Storytelling

Jon Cook
jon@keynotecontent.com

My name is Jon Cook. I am the founder of Keynote Content and I help mompreneurs like yourself craft stories into moolah-making, world-changing messages so you can stop struggling with how to communicate what makes you different, start changing someone else's life, and grow your business. My mission is to help rising thought leaders, such as speakers, coaches, and consultants, create and share remarkable messages for good.

The one thing every mompreneur needs to know when she's frustrated because her stories aren't connecting with her ideal client is to create an extraordinary story where your audience is the hero and you are their guide. **Here are 5 steps to help you do that.**

STEP 1: Identify Your Audience's Ordinary World
The legendary story architect Joseph Campbell is the one who introduced the Hero's Journey, a storyline you're familiar with, even if you may not realize it right now. A young hero finds herself in what we call her Ordinary World. She does the same thing or has the same type of experience day after day. Wherever the story takes place, the Ordinary World is her status quo. It's marked by some form of pain, suffering, confusion, or disconnect. Where she wants to be and where she is right now are worlds apart. She's a long way from being the hero in her story because she doesn't feel like the Hero in her story...yet.

If this story sounds familiar, this is the setting for the Hunger Games and a hundred other storylines like it. Katniss Everdeen is the hero in her Ordinary World. She sees the pain all around her. She senses a disconnect inside. She feels some form of suffering. Her mind and soul are confused and crave clarity to find out why she feels, thinks, and sees the way she does.

This is where your audience, your potential clients are right now. What's the status quo they're stuck in right now that you can step into with your story? There's also a chance that the people you want to serve don't even know they're stuck. A fish doesn't innately know it's in water - that's the only reality it's ever known. Your audience needs awareness.

They need to see their Ordinary World pales in comparison to the way things could be, not just the way they are right now. There's an Extraordinary World out there, a new reality, a better tomorrow that far surpasses their Ordinary World. They need to see the stark difference. How will they know unless you know what the two worlds look like for your audience?

Grab a piece of paper, set a timer on your phone for five minutes, draw two columns on your paper, and start writing everything you can think of about your audience's Ordinary World in the left-hand column. What does it feel like? What are the colors and shades associated with that world? What does it smell like? What are the light and dark places in their Ordinary World? Write as much as you can and be vividly descriptive.

Five minutes may feel like an eternity to you, but try to keep writing for a full five minutes. What are the words they're using to describe that world? How are they talking about what they wish was different about their everyday life? The more we can extract those exact words and feelings, the better we can define their current reality. If you've surveyed your subscriber list or client base before, grab their responses and see if you recognize patterns in their wording.

If your story isn't connecting with your audience, it's likely because you haven't found or don't understand their Ordinary World. This first step is about jumping into their world, both feet first, and planting your roots in their everyday experiences. That will give you solid ground to create a pathway your audience is aching to follow… and you can lead the way.

STEP 2: Introduce The Extraordinary World

What will it take for your audience to get out of their Ordinary World and headed towards an Extraordinary World? When your audience's pain of being stuck hurts more than the pain of changing their status quo, that's what ignites change. How do they know that what's out there is better and more fulfilling than their current reality unless you show them the difference?

If you're a fitness coach, it's showing them what their body could look like in 90 days. That's the before-and-after photos from other clients. That's the video testimonials. That's listing the negative emotions and thoughts they're experiencing right now and showing the damage those feelings and ideas are causing to every part of their life. When you open their eyes to the Extraordinary World, they can start exchanging those negative emotions and thoughts for positive, vibrant, healthy emotions and thoughts. The power is in knowing how our brains are wired for stories.

Our brains crave four main chemicals: dopamine, oxytocin, serotonin, and endorphins. These chemicals are hard-wired to activate specific feelings and experiences we crave. Dopamine is the strongest chemical our bodies can handle. It's what's connected to the most important desires coursing through our bodies. Love, success, fulfillment, power, intimacy, and acceptance are so incredibly attractive to us because our bodies desire the dopamine reaction of being seen as worthy of someone's time, attention, and energy. Dopamine is tied to the desire your audience wants to fulfill and you can help them experience that fulfillment through your story and what your business can offer them.

Oxytocin is what I call the love chemical because it's connected to being a part of something bigger than ourselves. We crave connection - a sense of belonging to a larger community. Your audience wants to know they're not alone. They need to know you're with them every step of the way on their journey towards their Extraordinary World.

Serotonin is the 'sunshine' chemical because it's closely tied to our sense of happiness and joy. That's why you may feel depressed or 'in a funk' on a cloudy day. Sunshine naturally activates and enhances serotonin production. How does your story bring more sunshine, more hope into your audience's life?

Endorphins may be the most easily misunderstood out of the four main brain chemicals. A lot of people think endorphins are what 'adrenaline junkies' chase. I used to think that until a neuroscientist showed me that endorphins are actually tied to that urge to do something heroic for the sake of someone else. What's the danger your audience is in that you can help save them from with your message?

Look at everything you wrote in the left-hand column on your paper in Step 1. Now, use the right-hand column and find a better alternative for every item in your left-hand column. For every emotion they're feeling, even good emotions, like "They feel successful," and find an even better emotion to replace that emotion. What you're doing is defining their Extraordinary World. Think about how their brains are craving more fulfillment, more connection, more happiness, and more heroic recognition right now.

STEP 3: Be The Guide, Not The Hero

Now, we call this the Hero's Journey, but as entrepreneurs, it's easy to fall into a trap. I've done this so many times it's almost laughable to me how easy it is to make this mistake. In the Hero's Journey, it's tempting to believe you are the hero in the story you're sharing with your audience.

You're not the hero - your audience is. You are the guide. You need to align your story with the spotlight on your audience first before you ever enter the story. When you do enter the story, you need to be positioned as the guide, not the hero.

In the Hunger Games, Haymitch is Katniss' guide. He's been in the arena, he knows what it takes to win, and he's connected with incredible resources and people to help her succeed. Of course, the stakes are much higher with Katniss than with our businesses, right? If Katniss doesn't succeed, she dies.

But, what if your story doesn't connect with your audience? What if the solution you have doesn't create the life-changing impact you *know* you can create? What will happen to your audience if *you* don't succeed?

If you're a health and wellness coach, it may mean people aren't getting the wellness transformation they need before they connect with you. What if it means more than that? What if it means your message helps someone avoid a heart attack? Your message could be more impactful than you can ever imagine. It's still up to your client to implement your solution, but your message has the power to save their life.

As the guide, you show them that they have the ability to implement everything you're showing them. What they lack is insight. They need to know what steps to take to successfully reach their Extraordinary World. It's a difficult journey with risks and dangers, but you know the way. You can show them the path to follow to go from their Ordinary World to the Extraordinary World.

This third step is all about positioning your role as your audience's guide in relation to their role as hero. Write out what your audience (potential guide) is trying to do on their own *without* your guidance. How would a hero try to reach the Extraordinary World *without* a guide? What missteps would they likely take and what would the consequences be for not relying on your expert assistance as their guide?

There are people in your audience already trying to do it on their own… and fabulously failing. This is what we call the Guided Outcome: what's the difference in the final outcome when people trust you to be their guide compared to when they try to do it all on their own? Write down what that Guided Outcome looks like. Be specific in your comparison. Reach deep into the emotional well to describe the difference between their "On My Own" outcome and your Guided Outcome. The gap between the two outcomes is what you can close as their guide.

STEP 4: Understand Their Dragon

"I can't possibly do that. It's too _____." Sound familiar? That's the voice of disbelief blocking your audience's path to their Extraordinary World. It's the fire-breathing dragon in the form of that sales presentation, product launch, life situation, or business decision. It's the greatest challenge your audience is staring right in the face. Your audience is already asking questions you can answer:

- Does your challenge appear larger than life? Yes.
- Is it scary? Absolutely.
- Can you overcome it? If you follow me, then yes.

Your story is about showing your audience how you faced that same challenge and succeeded. The challenge in front of your audience is feared by many who don't have a plan for overcoming it. This is what's keeping us on the couch or tucked away in our home office instead of making that offer. It's what intimidates us to postpone that sales presentation. It's what scares us into not taking that call or responding to that email. It's all a dragon and what do heroic stories teach us?

Dragons aren't meant to live long, especially when they meet the hero.

Have you ever seen a guide fighting the dragon for the hero? It makes for a terrible story because why wouldn't the guide just fight the dragon on their own instead of waiting for the hero to show up? Haymitch didn't step into the arena for Katniss because he'd already won his battle. Her hairdresser Effie didn't step into the arena because it wasn't her fight.

We all have our own dragons to fight, and in many cases, we start winning by being ourselves and recognizing the greatness inside. It takes grit, strength, love, and courage to face your greatest challenge. That's where your genius as the guide is most valuable. You don't have to give them those qualities - your audience already possesses them. As their guide it's your responsibility to help your audience awaken the courage, love, grit, and strength within to overcome their challenge.

What's the greatest challenge, the fire-breathing dragon, your audience is facing right now that's blocking the path to their Extraordinary World? While it's not your place or role to defeat the dragon, it's your job to understand its tactics, characteristics, and threats to your audience better than anyone else. It's time to define your audience's dragon.

Give it a specific name. Describe the feelings, thoughts, and reactions it's causing in the minds and hearts of your audience. Your audience needs to know that you understand their biggest challenge better than anyone else—and that you have a solution that will defeat their dragon.

Remember, this is about connecting your story with your audience. What have other 'guides' tried to do in the past that hasn't worked for your audience? What did you do when you faced a similar challenge that actually worked? What steps did you follow that led you to create your solution? Before you can offer your solution (that's the moolah-maker), you need to show you understand the challenge better than anyone else they know.

STEP 5: Align Your Solution With Their Extraordinary World

Besides not understanding your audience's Ordinary World, this may be the most overlooked part of connecting with your audience. This is the difference between "Oh, that's nice…" and "How can I work with you?" Many mompreneurs offer a solution without connecting that solution with their audience's journey towards the Extraordinary World. That's a profit-stopping mistake, and we're going to fix that with Step 5.

For the hero in the story, your prospective client, to actually overcome their challenge, what's the one solution you can offer that you know will work if they use it? What will open up the rest of the path for your audience and take them straight to their Extraordinary World? How do you know your solution works? What's the origin story for your solution? This may sound like, "I created (name of your program, product, or service) after seeing…."

There are opportunities all throughout your story to embed your solution. Whether it's a product, a service, coaching program, book, whatever your solution is, it needs to align with your audience's story and lead them to their Extraordinary World.

This is where all of the ideas, emotions, and desires we wrote down in the first few steps can help us craft a great solution. Chances are you already know what type of solution your audience needs, but the *format* of the solution usually doesn't matter. Books, blogs, videos, courses, these are just vehicles to deliver the solution you offer to your audience. Focus on the solution and desired outcome for your audience and weave those into your story.

How do you connect your solution with your audience's desired outcome (their Extraordinary World)? I like to emphasize three key words: "So you can _____."
If your audience is getting a template, what's the purpose? You could say, "You'll also receive a Business Development Blueprint for mapping out every part of

your day-to-day business so you can double your business in the next 90 days. *This is the resource I wish I had when I was where you are now on your journey.*"

Start including more "so you can" connecting points throughout your story. Translate your product into a great step for your prospective client to take towards their Extraordinary World. What does your product, service, or coaching do for their financial stability, time, stress level, or sense of accomplishment? Turn that transformation into part of your storyline.

If you want to stop struggling with what to say and better connect your story with your audience, you need to identify your audience's Ordinary World. You then invite them to see the exciting Extraordinary World that's waiting for them. You introduce yourself as a guide, not the hero, and show them you understand the fire-breathing dragon, that greatest challenge blocking the path to their Extraordinary World. Finally, you present a profitable, logical solution that will help them defeat their challenge and take them into their Extraordinary World. That's what will turn heads at cocktail parties and happy hours. That's what will leave your prospective client begging for your business card. That is the key to crafting your story into a moolah-making, world-changing message.

If you'd like my help crafting your money-making message, visit: m3clarity.com/story

Chapter 24

Raising Entrepreneurial Children

Julia Black

julia@explorium.co.uk

My name is Julia Black. I am an Educational Disruptor and Social Entrepreneur and I help mompreneurs give their children an entrepreneurial foundation that will allow them to live the life of their dreams AND make money from their passions. My mission is to help mompreneurs empower their children to be highly motivated, self-directed, switched-on learners with an entrepreneurial edge to help them succeed in life.

The one thing every mompreneur needs to know when she's worried about her children being happy and successful in life because they are totally bored and switched off from learning is that getting them engaged in their passions will unleash their entrepreneurial and creative spirit. **Here are 5 steps to help you do that.**

STEP 1: Shift Your Own Mindset First!

What most moms don't realize is that their child's growth potential, especially when it comes to raising entrepreneurial children, is limited by their own mindset. Think about this: You are their biggest role model, which means they are observing how you show up in life every single day. Your stories and limiting beliefs can become theirs too if you are not careful. Every mompreneur I work with quickly realizes that their child (often one, in particular, if they have more than one) is like a mirror to their own life reflecting back at them their own insecurities and self-doubt.

'Maybe I don't have what it takes to solve the problem of my child being SO BORED and disengaged at school.' 'Perhaps I'm not good enough to home educate them and get them excited to learn again.' What will my own parents think if I step away from convention and do things differently so my child can be happy, motivated, and successful in life?' Does this sound like you? Yep—almost every mompreneur I've worked with has at some point become aware of those thoughts in their head that are creating a glass ceiling on their own success. The bottom line is you have to increase your self-awareness and acknowledge the part you are contributing if you are to guide your children to their fullest potential.

Listen out for those persistent little ANTS (Automatic Negative Thoughts) that are crawling around in your brain running the show when it comes to your child's education. Record them in your journal and see how they are influencing the decisions you make on a daily basis. Get really good at tuning in to the emotions that come up for you around your own education.

To really lead your family on this entrepreneurial adventure, you have to see where your old-school thinking ('What if they don't get the grades? What if they don't get into college? What if I make the wrong decision?') is tripping you up. You need to move to much more illuminated thinking where you know, hand on heart, that you are doing EVERYTHING you can to unleash your child's fullest potential. To do that, you're going to have to start to think, act and BE different than the other moms on the playground. Remember your child's dreams are on the line here—so if that isn't enough motivation to kick out those beliefs and stories that have been holding you back all your life, then what is? You've probably already been doing this mindset work for your own business and now it's time to do it for your entrepreneurial children, so they can start learning how to make money from doing something that they love as soon as possible!

Commit to changing your story so you can spark that exponential growth potential that is inside your child. What other action steps can you take today that will make your child's education a more positive experience?

STEP 2: Learn From The Inside Out

This is where you get to draw out your child's natural born talent and superpower. Yep—every child is born with a gift to explore and if you are not careful, it will get 'educated' out of them FAST.

So with your new improved mindset (you are working on it, right?!) the one thing you need to know is that you can't help them step into their creative entrepreneurial spirit by trying to influence or change the external environment. So if that has been your strategy to date, you've been taking an 'outside-in approach' and it is going to set your child up for a big fall. It's important that your children adopt the habits of successful people, that their mindset (like yours) is strong, and they have the emotional resilience to fail, over and over again. In addition, it is essential that they are developing rock solid 21st century skills: Communication, Creativity, Collaboration, and Critical Thinking

Get your child learning from the 'inside-out' and then no matter where they find themselves in life, they will be able to learn, thrive, and flourish. I call this approach Lights On® because you can see it in their eyes—it is like their lights have come on. When your children are learning in this type of environment, you know they're on track to unleash their ultimate potential.

Your first action step to take is simple. Ask your child—if they could get up every morning and learn more about something, what would it be? What are they curious about? If it could be anything they want—what would they want to do? Then give them the opportunity to immerse themselves in what it is they love to do. This will encourage their natural born talent and passion to develop so they develop a love of learning.

STEP 3: Set Up A Learning Portfolio

To prepare your child for the rapidly changing world they are growing up in, it's important for your child to understand what they are capable of achieving beyond their grades. Now, most parents fall into the trap of thinking that learning is linear, because our traditional education model is designed around a chronological age. However, as a mompreneur you know that real-life learning, the kind you need to succeed as an entrepreneur, is messy. It has ups and downs, stops and starts, forward momentum and backward steps. Your child's learning portfolio needs to reflect that adventure and document a true account of their growth and capability as they become expert learners over time. It's been said that 10,000 hours leads to skill mastery. With this in mind, the earlier you start the better. When you get your child learning through their passions and tapping into those superpowers they have, they can absolutely clock up those hours towards mastery before they've even entered their teens.

Notice whether they are creating or consuming. Are they doing something with the information they are soaking up or are they just soaking up information? Your goal is to have them create and not just consume. It is in the creation that the passion for learning is sparked.

You want to encourage your children to begin creating original content. It might be creative writing or a film they are producing, or maybe it is artwork. Perhaps they are taking apart some old technology and repurposing the parts. Take note of times when they are birthing an idea that comes to fruition. This is your starting point and their evidence of what they are capable of achieving when they are committed to following through.

STEP 4: Get Them Wired For Learning

This next step is really where the BIG entrepreneurial growth starts to happen for your child as you begin to get them, what I call, 'Wired For Learning.'

By now you understand that when your child is motivated, curious, and loving learning from the inside out, deep learning will begin and you will see their truest potential start to shine through. Because you've shifted your own mindset and dumped your old-school thinking, you are now able to focus in on what matters: getting your child's lights shining brightly so they can learn in a way that supports them in the 21st century. Because here's the thing—if your child's lights are off, they simply cannot learn. Chances are, if you have a natural born entrepreneur in the house, they will already be showing signs of resistance to sitting still all day at school and to the typical learning schedule. Unfortunately, when school is a struggle, many parents are compelled to get their child diagnosed and assigned a label. Instead, I want to encourage you to see these signs as a great opportunity that should be nurtured.

My father was a highly successful social entrepreneur who was awarded the honor of a CBE by the British Queen. He was also the naughtiest boy in his school! He didn't read until he was 15 (he was dyslexic) and the psychologist wrote him off as never likely to accomplish anything. He was a rebel for sure, and I like to think of him as a rebel with a cause. He was able to use his conceptual mind to his advantage and tap into his natural entrepreneurial and creative spirit. The way his brain was wired was his superpower. All too often, it is only when children are struggling within the school environment that parents begin to question how they learn. I encourage you, even if you have a child who can learn the traditional way, to make sure you consider how your child learns best. Are they a visual learner? Or kinesthetic? Do they have a tendency to be an introverted thinker or do they need to externalize their thoughts to help them learn? Do they give up when they reach an obstacle or do they have a really strong learning mindset?

As they begin to learn through creative passion projects, there will be so many growth potential opportunities for your child. Your child's brain is literally a work-in-progress and, as a result of their everyday experiences, is constantly being rewired. This includes the amount of mistakes and obstacles they face, the inputs they consume, and the outputs they create. If we don't help create these opportunities for them, then they are not using their brain's neuroplasticity to their advantage. During adolescence, a lot of neural pruning takes place so the neural networks that are not used fade away. If they are only passive learners, can you imagine the opportunities they are missing out on? Their critical thinking will be diminished as they are not developing that muscle. Are they growing those neural networks that enable them to think on their feet? There are many ways your child's current style of learning could be limiting their brain's potential and, as a result, limiting their entrepreneurial potential.

The exciting thing is that as soon as you commit to giving your children plenty of opportunities to learn, their brains will naturally grow. What new areas can you commit to exploring with your child?

STEP 5: Include Your Whole Family

It is time to start to really look at your child's education as an investment in your whole family's transformational growth. You can't raise entrepreneurial kids in a half-hearted way, because while they might have great ideas, there's a lot that goes into developing the skill set and mindset necessary to convert an idea into money.

Does your child have what it takes to commit to an idea and go all in, no matter what? Maybe not right now, but just imagine what opportunities open up for you as a family with your renewed commitment to aligning your own entrepreneurial adventure with your child's education! Both of my teenagers are entrepreneurs with their own online courses. My 16-year-old daughter has a course teaching 6-12 year olds how to write creative short stories and my 13-year-old son teaches 6-12 year olds to become filmmakers.

As I grew as an entrepreneur, I made sure they did too. They watched me make the time and financial investment necessary to develop my own skills. They saw me be vulnerable and cry when all I wanted to do was give up and quit. They saw me have the courage to do things that filled me with fear because I had a mission and a vision that pulled me forward.

So, what you need to do now is get clear on your vision for your family's learning adventure and commit to it. Raising entrepreneurial children is a whole-family commitment—so go all in, even when it gets tough. Even when it's difficult to get your children off their screens to work on their passion project and they resist or give you push back, just hold firm and go back to looking at what mindset blocks come up for you. 'Maybe I don't have what it takes to do this?' Of course you do! If you need to, invest in a coach who supports you to develop the mindset and skill set to keep on going, no matter what.

The exciting thing is that as soon as you commit to rewiring your family's brains, the fun begins! Build in fun, creative challenges into your week for your family to do together. Why? Because, when you become a learner alongside them, you have the opportunity to create a family culture that values curiosity, exploration, and creativity.

I love helping mompreneurs learn how to create a culture of 21st century learning in their homes so they can impact their children's growth potential. My expertise is in working with mompreneurs to ensure that their children are learning through their passions so they can be financially rewarded doing something that they love.

If you'd like to learn more, visit: www.explorium.co.uk/ready

Congratulations!

After reading the strategies offered by these leading experts, I'm certain you have been inspired and found answers. My hope is that you've begun to take action and have started seeing results!

If you'd like even more support and guidance and are curious about working with me, I invite you to schedule a complimentary call to see how I can help you fast track your success.

As the Founder of Big Money Business Builder and The Parenting System Training and Coaching Solutions, my expertise is in helping you create, grow and develop the 6 figure business of your dreams in ways that are fast, simple, maximize your impact and make you the most money - so that you can have it all - without sacrificing your sanity.

To schedule your complimentary call with me, please go to:
www.bigmoneybusinessbuilder.com/yes

www.ingramcontent.com/pod-product-compliance
Lightning Source LLC
Chambersburg PA
CBHW070335220526
45467CB00001B/136